# The Sacred Oasis

1. Wei period: Cave 272 (P188/J), West Wall. *See page* 66
Central Buddha sculpture in alcove, head, chest and arms restored. Circular alcove, comparatively rare at Ch'ien Fo Tung, contains paintings of attendant bodhisattvas interspersed with flowers. Haloes and aureole unretouched

# THE SACRED OASIS

*Caves of the Thousand Buddhas*
*Tun Huang*

by

IRENE VONGEHR VINCENT

*with a preface by*
PEARL BUCK

THE UNIVERSITY OF CHICAGO PRESS
CHICAGO ILLINOIS

*First published in mcmliii*
*by Faber and Faber Limited*
*24 Russell Square London W.C. 1*
*Printed in Great Britain by*
*R. MacLehose and Company Limited*
*The University Press Glasgow*

*Published in the United States of America by*
*The University of Chicago Press,*
*Chicago 37, Illinois*

*This book*
*is affectionately dedicated*
*to*
JOHN BENJAMIN VINCENT

# Preface

This book is the record of an extraordinary pilgrimage. The pilgrim was a young American woman who had made a vow to herself, years before, that she would, life permitting, see with her own eyes the sacred Buddhist temple caves at Tun Huang on the far borders of China. The place where she made the vow was a prosaic classroom in an American college. But China was not so far as it might have been, for the young woman had been born in China and while she was in college some remembered vision had led her to take a course in ancient Chinese art, during which she learned of the Tun Huang caves.

Later, in 1948, she was living in Peking, then the wife of a young American. They had two children, and life was full enough, one would think. But the vow was still in her heart, and her husband was wise enough to urge her to fulfil it. He would, he said, take care of the children, with the help of the good Chinese nurse.

Thus supported and encouraged, the young woman went on her pilgrimage. It was a long way. She flew as far as she could, and there were still eight hundred miles to go, each mile much longer than a mile because the roads were rough and the vehicle was a crowded truck. And a crowded truck in China is ten times as crowded as a truck can be anywhere else. At night she laid herself down on a brick bed and slept. Her food was the ordinary baked bread of North West China and, I suppose, the garlic which is often rolled into it, but such was her pilgrim's ardour that she declared it delicious.

The end of the pilgrimage was at Tun Huang, that sandy city in the desert, the gateway to China from India and Central Asia. Through this gate Buddhist missionaries, in the first century after Christ, came from India into China, bearing their gospel of a gentle and selfless religion. Here they paused again on their homeward way and here they began the vast shrine which endures until this day. It is a meeting place of the art of India, Central Asia and China. The sacred caves, man made, are carved into a rocky cliff that rises above a stream of water, and one chapel leads into another, each decorated with mural paintings and sculpture.

The pilgrim stayed much longer than she should have, she says, for though she was mindful of the little family who had bravely allowed her to come, yet she was so bewitched and so bemused by the surpassing beauty of what she saw that, like Paul of old, she did not know whether she was in the body or out of it.

She made a great many photographs, and hitch-hiked her way back to Lanchow again, and thence to Peking. When the family returned to the United States the following year, she learned from her former professor that she had 'valuable new information', and that her photographs should be published.

# Preface

'With the heartening encouragement of my husband,' she writes me, 'and the grudging co-operation of my children (both put up with cooking of a spartan simplicity for a year), I finally completed a text.'

The text is good. It is fresh and informing, and also accurate. The photographs are well chosen. One wishes that they might all have been in colour, but that would have made this book impossibly expensive. There are thirty or forty masterpieces in the Tun Huang temple caves, 'true works of art', the author says, 'which will some day take their place in the catalogue of great Buddhist art. . . . The Tun Huang murals include the only extant Wei and perhaps the largest collection of authentic T'ang wall paintings in existence.'

Yet strangely few of our experts in Asian art have seen these masterpieces, for few have made the pilgrimage. Many know them only through Pelliot's monochrome photographs made in 1908. A notable exception is Langdon Warner, who has visited the caves and is as enthusiastic about them as Mrs. Vincent is.

At any rate, we who have never made the pilgrimage must thank her for sharing with us this great adventure.

PEARL BUCK

# Contents

# Illustrations

*The cave numbers given below are those of the Tun Huang Institute. The Pelliot numbers follow in parenthesis.*

# Illustrations

## Illustrations

# Illustrations

# Acknowledgement

A great many people helped me both on my journey and in preparing this book, and I record my thanks to them here.

Especially I must mention Mrs. Ching-yi Dougherty who helped me with the Chinese translations, Dr. Ferdinand Lessing who explained many points of Buddhist iconography, Mrs. Lovena de Shelly who aided me in the disagreeable job of checking the various numbering systems used in the caves, and Professor James Plumer of the University of Michigan, from whom I first heard of the caves, and who urged me to write about them after I saw them. Dr. LeRoy Davidson of Yale University and his wife, who both read the manuscript, and Dr. Richard Aldrich of the University of Miami, an expert on the caves, have been most helpful. To Professor Langdon Warner I owe much for his illuminating interpretations of Tun Huang's history and art. He is the 'noted American scholar' I have mentioned several times.

I can never sufficiently thank the good people of Kansu who assumed charge of me, a stranger in their province, nor my husband, John B. Vincent, whose observations and color pictures of the wall-paintings, made on a later trip, were a valuable aid to memory.

PART ONE

# The Sacred Oasis: A Task of Sixteen Centuries

CHAPTER I

# The Overland Roads: Eastward Path of Buddhism to China

For centuries, the front gate to China lay on her west, the landward side. The Pacific Ocean was, in ancient days, a natural Great Wall which protected—and often isolated—her on the east. On the west, beyond the man-made Great Wall of mud-brick, lay the great roads, perhaps the oldest in the world, to Central Asia, India, the Middle East and Europe. The roads, ribbons of earth beaten to a stone-like hardness by the feet of men and pack-animals, traversed the lofty mountains, broad prairies, fertile oases and vast deserts of the 'land of passage'—Inner Asia—which stretches from the Black Sea to the Yellow River, from the steppes of Siberia to the snow-covered Himalayas.

On this vast stage were enacted mighty dramas of history which influenced and altered profoundly the countries joined by the roads or through which they passed. Within this immense zone, the civilized empires tried to contain the 'barbarians' or to reach out and subdue them. The 'barbarians' themselves, of many tribes and races—such as the Huns, Turks, and Mongols—thrust out from here over the centuries to harass or conquer the great civilizations, which attracted them as irresistibly as the moon draws the tides.

The inner Asian roads were military highways over which thundered the armies of many peoples in a blood-stained pattern of invasion, conquest and migration. They were highways of trade, crossed and recrossed by merchant-caravans laden with the silks of China, the spices of India, the jade of Central Asia. Most important perhaps, they were the arteries through which spread the arts and religions of the lands at the periphery, to intermingle, to transform and be transformed.

About two thousand years ago, four great civilizations had arisen in a semi-circle around Inner Asia. At the extreme east was the mighty empire of China under the Han rulers, whose proud name the Chinese use to-day when they distinguish themselves from the tribal or border peoples of their country. Westward were the highly developed cultures of the Indian, Iranian and Graeco-Roman worlds, to which China was linked—directly and indirectly—by the web of the overland roads. These resembled a many-strand necklace on which were hung, like precious beads, the oasis-cities of Central Asia, or 'Serindia'. In these oases, like gardens in the desert, bloomed the hybrid flowers—nevertheless beautiful or interesting—of the civilizations which, at various times or simultaneously, had nourished them. Into the soil of the late—or 'belated'—classicism of the hellenized culture which flourished on the trade routes was implanted the seed of Buddhism. Indian and Iranian influences were the vitalizing sun

2. Our truck refused to move. No one dismounts unless the halt will be for half an hour or more

5. Approach to Ch'ien Fo Tung. The path down the cliff is in the foreground, the gate to the right. Through the trees left of the gate is Abbot Wang's temple. A few streams trickle through the river bed; on the opposite bank are a number of small stupas and, in the distance, the Nan Shan

and rain which brought to fruition their religious arts, and these were to serve, largely, as the first patterns followed by China when Buddhism there was a new religion demanding new forms of artistic expression.

The Inner Asian roads were one of the three or four main channels through which the creed of Buddhism flowed from India to neighbouring lands, to produce, when it was absorbed and fused to their own traditions, a great flowering of the human spirit and the arts. Almost all of Asia, for several centuries, was spiritually united in a Buddhist world which extended at one time from Afghanistan to Japan, from India to Java. The common language of this world was Sanskrit, as Latin was to become the language of Christendom. Even to-day, when Buddha is no longer worshipped in his mother-land of India, and when Islam and other beliefs reign in many of the former Buddhist kingdoms, his name is revered by millions of men and women, who form perhaps a third part of the human race.

The historical Buddha, later known as Gautama or Sākyamuni, was born in the north-east of India during the sixth century before Christ. His gentle message—in essence, one of compassion towards all living creatures and of how they might escape the fate-ordained cycle of endless rebirths—had been at first a plea to return to a purer Hinduism than that of his day. But, in time, he became deified and surrounded by a host of divine beings veiled in legends, and worshipped through the hierarchy and rituals of a separate faith, rooted, however, in the essential tenets of Hinduism. For this reason, although Buddhism for centuries overshadowed its mother-religion in India, it was finally re-absorbed by the faith which had, in a sense, given it birth.

## The Overland Roads

To his followers in the religious communities he had founded, Gautama Buddha entrusted the propagation of his doctrine. In India, it flourished and became widespread under the imperial patronage of the great King Ashoka in the third century B.C. A royal saint, whose name was later honoured throughout Asia, Ashoka was converted to Buddhism after he had completed the bloody conquest—begun by his grandfather—of almost all India. Repenting bitterly the carnage which had gained him the empire, Ashoka ordered to be carved on stone columns and rocks the precepts of Buddhism, simply stated, that his people might learn them. These columns, which remain among the earliest known examples of Buddhist art, enjoined the people—'his children'—to love one another, to respect all religious sects, to be kind to animals. It is interesting that the motif of one of his columns—the lion of Sarnāth—is to-day the official seal of the young Republic of India.

Ashoka built stupas to house sacred relics, founded great monastery-universities, built hostels for the poor and hospitals for men and animals. The kingdom became so peaceful that it was said a woman might safely travel alone the length and breadth of the kingdom with a jewel in her hand.

This zealous emperor, 'the beloved of the gods,' whose realm had contacts with the countries of the Mediterranean and Middle East through trade and embassies, sent abroad missionaries to spread the Buddhist gospel. Tradition says his own son carried the Doctrine to Ceylon, which to-day remains the spiritual head of one important division—the Hīnayāna or Lesser Vehicle—of Buddhism. This church, as recently as 1944, showed its strength when it caused a wealthy and important Indian motion picture company to halt production on a film of Buddha's life, a project it feared would be handled sacrilegiously.

It is believed that Ashoka's missionaries were instrumental in converting to Buddhism the peoples who inhabited north-western India—the present-day Afghanistan, Kashmir and the Punjāb. From the name of a province in the Kābul Valley of Afghanistan, this region is often loosely called Gandhāra. Gandhāra, from the ardour of its converts and from its pivotal position astride the trade-routes between the Middle East, India and Central Asia, was to become a sort of second Holy Land of Buddhism.

India was, of course, the fountain-head, the first Holy Land where the fortunate sites which had seen the great events of Buddha's life—his birth, enlightenment, first sermon and death—became sacred shrines, as did other places where, it was said, Buddha had returned to earth in former births, as an elephant, a deer, a hare and so on. In India, Buddhism had continued to thrive, developing its great monasteries and centres of learning, its art and iconography, its canon of scripture, its rituals and legends. Missionaries and teachers departed in great numbers to carry the Law, to translate the scriptures for other lands. Gandhāra was to be a point of departure for Buddhism in its eastward progress through Central Asia to China, and thence to Korea and Japan.

Alexander the Great had invaded Bactria and north-west India in the fourth century before Christ, and it was partly to counter his attacks that the Mauryan empire of Ashoka's grandfather had come to power. Alexander had been forced to withdraw, but groups of

Greek colonists and adventurers remained behind, establishing strong states in Bactria. Nearby Gandhāra, lying at the cross-roads, was to be repeatedly invaded by them and by others, and became a receptacle into which poured cultural stimuli from several civilizations—Greek, Roman, Iranian, and Indian.

During the first century B.C., Gandhāra became for a time the seat of a powerful empire under the Kushāns, dominant of several tribes called Indo-Scythians by European historians and Yüeh-chih by the Chinese. Their power extended over most of Central Asia and northern India.

The Kushāns, a people believed to be of Indo-European stock, had originally migrated from the region of the present-day Kansu province of China. Once established, after many wanderings, in north-western India, they adopted and fostered the heterogeneous arts and cultures they found in their empire. The ruling house became zealous patrons of Buddhism; its greatest ruler, Kanishka, was later, like Ashoka, revered throughout the Buddhist world. These monarchs constructed great temples and sent out missionaries who established Buddhism in the oases to the east.

The Kushān period, spanning more than two centuries, was part of an age of extraordinary cultural and religious ferment. In distant Galilee, Christ, founder of another world-religion, was born. Within the Kushān empire, not only were the art forms of the Buddhist religion further developed, but the type of Buddhism which was to triumph in north-eastern Asia—the Mahāyāna or Great Vehicle—was expanded into a more or less complete system, undoubtedly influenced

4. First view of Ch'ien Fo Tung after passing through the north gate. Sand covers the cliff top like a roof, above which can be seen the tower of the Nine Storey Building

5. A view of the cliff and chapels. The Nine Storey Building is on the right. The lines of two verandahs built by the Tun Huang Institute appear in the left-hand portion. The ante-chapels here have been partially destroyed

6. Central portion of the caves, showing four levels of chapels. One timbered stucco ante-chapel, to the left of the tree, is intact, as is one just above it. The staircase visible at the extreme right leads from a *p'ai lou*, or archway, called Ku Han Ch'iao, the Ancient Han bridge, reckoned the centre of the cave-chapels

7. Close up of a damaged chapel (*See page 75*), its shape typical of the majority of chapels both large and small, and even of the inside, about two feet high, of some of the stupas on the east bank of the river bed. The projecting wall at right is all that remains of its ante-chapel. Fragments of wall painting retain some pigment despite decades of exposure to sun

by intellectual currents from neighbouring lands, and later to be elaborated and modified by China, Japan and Tibet.

The earliest portrayals of Buddha in human form that have been discovered so far are the works of what became the two principal art centres of the Kushān empire. These were, in the north, the 'Hellenistic school' of Gandhāra, which reflected in the course of its growth the various artistic streams which flowed into it; the other, towards the south, was the 'Indian school' of Mathurā. Many influences, both foreign and indigenous, had affected either centre; each, undoubtedly, interacted, to a greater or lesser extent, on the other. In the end, the southern forms, even before flowering into the great art of India's Gupta period (fourth to sixth centuries A.D.) transformed and 'Indianized' the Gandhāra school. As it has been expressed, 'Greece smothered in the embrace of India.'

Buddhist works—carved railings, sculptures and reliefs—older than either of the Kushān schools have survived, and it appears that, for long after Buddha's death, Indian artists did not depict him in the likeness of a man, in part because he could not be conceived anthropomorphically if he had attained Nirvāna. In illustrating the events of his life, artists represented him either by blank space or by such symbols as a wheel, a pair of footprints, Sanskrit letters. Nor is it known for certain when and by whom the first images of the Buddha in human shape were made, in that form which is found—in stone and plaster, in metal and on silk and paper—throughout the Buddhist world. With the chignon or 'protuberance of wisdom' on the head, the elongated ear-lobes stretched by the jewels that had been cast away, the *ūrnā* or forehead dot and other 'signs', the body wrapped in the draped robes of a monk, this conception of a Buddha—although showing many variations—preserves everywhere unmistakable similarities that point to a common source of origin.

Perhaps time—and archaeology—may reveal the arch-type of the Buddha image, and so settle the controversy over whether it was the Gandhāran artists, steeped in Greek anthropomorphic tradition, or Indian artists, imbued with the equally anthropomorphic traditions of Hinduism, who first fashioned in stone and plaster their conception, to be adopted universally, of the 'Enlightened One'.

Proceeding from India, Buddhism had gradually completed the peaceful conquest of Central Asia, where there developed a religious art which, if mostly 'borrowed', had been absorbed by native genius and taste to produce an art truly Central-Asian. Several centres on the trade-routes there became, in themselves, strongholds of Buddhist learning with famous monasteries, the destination of many a pilgrim or scholar who ventured no further. It was natural that China should turn to these neighbouring centres, as well as to India herself and such images and paintings as the pilgrims brought home, for instruction in the Doctrine and the art forms it required.

It is not clear when the first word of Buddhism reached China. Some missionaries and lay-believers appear to have ventured to the coast of China by the sea-routes in the third century before our era. An account of this faith, together with images and texts, seems to have reached the Han emperors a century later from the Kushāns, or Yüeh-chih, with whom the Han rulers tried to form alliances against the increasing power of the Huns, traditional enemies of both, who had originally driven the Yüeh-chih from their Kansu homelands.

In A.D. 68, an Indian missionary, Kāsyapa Matānga, at the request of the Han emperor, crossed by the overland route to reach the Chinese capital with Buddhist scriptures, and this date is usually accepted as the entry of Buddhism into China. Matānga was followed by more missionaries and translators, both Indian and Central Asian, and for the next three centuries, despite occasional reverses, Buddhism increasingly won converts among the peoples of China. Perhaps they were unusually receptive to this religion because generations of political turmoil and warfare had followed the decline of the Han empire in the third century A.D.

By the fifth century, most of north China had been consolidated into the Wei empire of alien tribes, the Tobas, who gave it some stability for the first time in over three centuries. The Tobas adopted Chinese culture, which had behind it centuries of development. To the art, which had already been brought to a high point, and especially to the sculpture, considered by many the greatest in Chinese history, they may have brought certain qualities of their own, something of the vigour of their nomad background. The Wei rulers ardently supported Buddhism, and not only patronized the monasteries, but took the lead in constructing lavish new temples.

CHAPTER II

# The 'Port of Entry'; Tun Huang Oasis

The oasis of Tun Huang, at the extreme west of Kansu province was the 'port of entry' for Buddhist missionaries of the 'western regions' and India who travelled to China by the overland roads. It was the last Chinese outpost, where Chinese pilgrims and merchants fitted themselves out for the long journey west. Even before the Wei period, Tun Huang was already a very old garrison city and trading centre, dating at least to the Han dynasty, and where ruins of Han fortifications, once a vital link in the chain of western defences, may be seen to-day. Tun Huang's name, which means 'Blazing Beacon', is a revival of the ancient Han name for the site, three centuries ago replacing its other, Sha Chow. Tun Huang must long have enjoyed a certain importance from its position in a natural corridor between Central Asia and China.

It was perhaps inevitable that one of the greatest Buddhist shrines should arise in the vicinity of Tun Huang, where Buddhism had early penetrated Chinese soil. Here returning and departing travellers met,

8. Northern group of caves, beyond the oasis, believed to have been the monks' quarters. Accumulated sand on the cliff top equals in height the exposed portion of cliff

9. Wei period sculpture: Cave 249 (P101), West wall. *See page* 75
Central Buddha in alcove. Head and hands of this figure are restored, but wall painting is original

the one thankful to have completed safely a perilous journey, the other anxious for protection from the dangers ahead.

The shrine was not built, as one might expect, on the oasis of Tun Huang itself, where were situated the officials' headquarters, the caravanserais, the inns and markets. The great temple was to be found across the sterile sands to the south, where a stream ran beside a rock cliff. About twelve miles from Tun Huang, this was the largest and most conveniently located of several such cliffs in the area.

This tiny oasis was known popularly as Ch'ien Fo Tung, the Caves of the Thousand Buddhas. It is the sacred oasis of our title, and was to become one of the glories of Buddhism. The cluster of man-made caves carved here would endure long after the mud-brick walls and dwellings of Tun Huang had been levelled at least once and rebuilt at nearly the same site.

Carving temples into living rock goes back to remotest antiquity. Among other places, it may have originated in India. From here, the oasis-cities of Central Asia probably copied it, for this imported style of building suited the peculiar conditions of their terrain, and from Central Asia it was imitated by the Chinese.

The oasis-cities, their precious fields ringed by arid desert, could not produce the great timber, and they had not the stone necessary for the long-lasting structures which people all over the world demand for their temples. However, nearby in the desert are often found outcroppings of rock, which, if it cannot be quarried, can be hollowed out to make rooms. Free-standing mud-brick and wooden temples were built also, but few have survived the fierce winds, drifting sands and frequent wars of this area. Because of the wars, caves might also provide some additional protection for the holy books, statues and paintings; perhaps even for the priests themselves in times of religious persecution. A chain of these Buddhist rock-cut chapels seems to have extended from India through Central Asia at least as far as the mountains south of Kanchow in Kansu, and besides these, cave-temples are found in many other parts of China.

An inscribed stone tablet of the T'ang dynasty, preserved at Ch'ien Fo Tung, states that the first chapel—the 'Cave of Unequalled Height'— was constructed by an Indian monastic, called Lo Ts'un, in what corresponds to A.D. 366. The name of this earliest chapel, in Chinese *Moa Kao K'u*, is now often used to designate the site of Ch'ien Fo Tung, although it is not known whether what is now the highest of the cave-chapels is actually the one first excavated by Lo Ts'un, who may have been inspired by the gigantic Buddha of Bamīyān in Afghanistan.

For some decades after this, the small oasis was probably dependent for its support on the passing traders and pilgrims who might come from Tun Huang to worship briefly at the new shrine and give alms to the few priests in charge.

During the Wei ascendancy of the fifth and sixth centuries in China or, as it is also called, the Six Dynasties period, a large number of chapels were excavated and decorated at Ch'ien Fo Tung, of which about twenty-three remain more or less intact. It is known that more were carved at this time, for recent research reveals that wall-paintings of the Wei period lie under the plaster and murals of later years.

## The 'Brilliant Era'

In the sculptures and paintings of the earliest chapels of Ch'ien Fo Tung, the influences of the Central Asian and Indian models are most clearly seen. Possibly foreign artists were imported or itinerant painters—known to have plied their trade on the roads—were engaged to paint parts or even the whole of the walls. Local craftsmen may have been sent abroad to study the new religious art, or perhaps it was a combination of these.

Yet, in the portions of the wall-paintings where iconographic demands were less strict—such as in some of the ceiling and border designs, the human or animal figures of the *jātaka* narrative-pictures of Buddha's previous births, and in the donors' portraits, we see an art that seems to be in the Chinese tradition, as it had developed until then.

Three and a half centuries of the divided and frequently warring states of China after the downfall of the Hans were brought to an end when the country was unified under the short-lived Sui dynasty (A.D. 580–618). Paving the way for the magnificent achievements of the T'ang empire which followed, this was a time of transition whose abundant artistic activity, mirrored in a large number of cave-chapels at Ch'ien Fo Tung, was in part the link between the jaunty vigour of the Wei chapels, with their foreign and native elements, and the balanced complexity and clarity of the T'ang, typically Chinese.

The T'ang era has been called the 'most brilliant' in Chinese history. The whole of China was consolidated under their rule, Korea subdued, and Chinese political power extended perhaps as far as the Caspian Sea when the Central Asian oases were made vassals or tributary states of the T'ang empire. The T'ang armies even halted for a time the triumphant eastward march of the Arabs, when these newly converted and fiery followers of Mohammed—a sword in one hand, the Koran in the other—swept into Inner Asia.

A splendid court at Ch'ang An, the modern Si An, received embassies from the rulers of the north Indian states, Persia and even from Byzantium, then at the height of its power. Not only was there free intercourse between China and the lands to the west, but the Chinese showed great interest and often deep admiration for the arts and ideals of foreign countries. In the capital and elsewhere, there were not only flourishing and wealthy Buddhist monasteries—for this was the great age of Buddhism in China—but the followers of Nestorian Christianity, Zoroastrianism, Mohammedanism, Judaism, and Manichaeism were permitted to build their temples, and this spirit of tolerance was due very largely to the Buddhists.

Out of the vigorous intellectual ferment of the age grew a number of Chinese Buddhist 'schools' or sects, some strongly influenced by Taoism, which were to retain their form, with some exceptions, to the present day, and among which were the forms accepted during this period by Korea and Japan. Of these sects, the two most important were the 'Pure Land' school, centred around the worship of the Buddha Amitābha and his 'Paradise of the West', a doctrine of salvation by faith; the other was the Ch'an (in Japanese, Zen) sect, which aspired to enlightenment through contemplation or the 'sudden flash' of intuition.

From this time also, there streamed toward Central Asia a reverse flow of Chinese art and culture, of which

10. Wei period: Cave 249 (P101), West wall.
Detail of central Buddha of plate 9, the view seen by a kneeling worshipper

11. Wei period: Cave 249 (P101). *See pages* 86, 87

Ceiling of chapel. 'Lantern roof' design painted on central panel. Eleven-headed beast to extreme left, human figures mounted on or drawn by mythical animals. Crenellated gate partly visible at right

many remains have been found in the oasis-cities of eastern Central Asia, or Chinese Turkestan as it is also called.

Ch'ien Fo Tung had been, at first, a way-point on the path to India and Gandhāra. But, during this period and perhaps even earlier, it became in itself an object of pilgrimage. Chinese travellers also continued to visit India and the western countries, to retrace the footsteps of the Buddha, to worship at famous shrines, to obtain images and copies of the scriptures and to study at the feet of erudite Indian teachers.

This was a long, although occasionally interrupted, period of prosperity for Ch'ien Fo Tung, which continued even after the T'ang power was shattered. The community of monks increased and gradually there was accumulated an extensive library in Sanskrit, the languages of Central Asia, Tibetan and Chinese. Many monks were engaged in the arduous task of translating the scriptures into Chinese; at least one wrote a widely-used commentary, and a great centre of learning grew up where members of several Buddhist sects, and perhaps even of other religions important in the area, lived and studied together.

We know that a pious military officer, stationed near here during the early T'ang dynasty, begged Hsüan Tsang, the 'T'ang monk', to end at Ch'ien Fo Tung his proposed—and officially forbidden—journey to India, for here would be teachers and scriptures to satisfy him for years. Hsüan Tsang refused and continued on his way, for he was passionately eager to worship at the great shrines of India and Gandhāra, and to return to China with scriptures and knowledge which would settle forever doctrinal matters misunderstood in China.

However, many years later, on his journey home, the famous 'Master of the Law' left some of his hard-won manuscripts at Ch'ien Fo Tung and spent some months there. These very books were to play, after a lapse of some twelve centuries, an important and romantic role in what was at once the recovery and dispersal of the library.

A large corps of artists and craftsmen presumably lived at Ch'ien Fo Tung, whose task was to build and decorate new chapels, fashion sculptures, and paint the banners and votive offerings needed by pilgrims and the religious community. It is possible also that lay artists were commissioned to decorate chapels—it is recorded that many T'ang artists painted religious subjects—or they may actually have lived at Ch'ien Fo Tung for extended periods. Many wall-paintings of secular subjects at Ch'ien Fo Tung seem to show more skill and attention to worldly matters than might be expected from monks trained in painting. It appears that the artists and workmen of Ch'ien Fo Tung were sometimes loaned to the smaller neighbouring communities, for several lesser groups of cave-chapels nearby show strong similarities to the chapels of Ch'ien Fo Tung. Of these, Wan Fo Hsia (Caves of the Myriad Buddhas) in the Ansi region have been partly studied by Chinese and western scholars. Other less well-known cave-temples in Kansu are: Hsi Ch'ien Fo Tung and Tung Ch'ien Fo Tung (Western and Eastern Thousand Buddha Caves) near Yü Men, east of Tun Huang, and more distant, Hung Shan Sse at Shih Chin; Wen Shu Shan near Chiu Ch'uan, and Ma T'i Sse in the Kan-chow area. These, with Ch'ien Fo Tung, the most important, are six of at least eight groups of rock-cut chapels known to exist in Kansu.

## Invasions by 'Barbarians'

Together with the larger oasis of Tun Huang, Ch'ien Fo Tung probably became self-supporting, materially and spiritually during the T'ang period, and may even have been the seat of a Buddhist bishop whose authority covered a large if not populous see. When the T'ang power began to decline in the west during the mid-ninth century, Ch'ien Fo Tung still prospered. The oasis of Tun Huang, believed to have been even larger than it is to-day, came for two centuries under the rule of local noble families, the Chang and later the Ts'ao. Upon the construction of cave-chapels, they and their relatives lavished much wealth, and the largest chapels, immense halls in size, date from this time.

As a modern Chinese account says, 'such good fortune could not last'. Tun Huang was threatened from the south by the Tangguts, tribes of Tibetan origin. Early in the eleventh century, probably in anticipation of this feared 'barbarian' invasion, the great library of Ch'ien Fo Tung, with its manuscripts and block-printed rolls as well as a large number of temple banners and paintings, was hidden—in evident haste—in a small chapel and walled up. The monastic community seems to have dispersed for a time, and the secret hiding place was not only concealed from Tangguts but, for many centuries, from the world.

CHAPTER III

# The Shrine: Caves of the Thousand Buddhas

Tun Huang and its environs became a part of the Hsi Hsia empire of the Tangguts, and Ch'ien Fo Tung's importance, at least as a centre of learning, seems to have declined. It remained a venerated shrine, however. A number of new caves were carved and older ones repainted or restored, although how many of either is not yet known.

From the end of the fourth century to the early part of the thirteenth, when the Tangguts were defeated by the Mongols, it is believed that the majority of cave-temples at Ch'ien Fo Tung—estimated at nearly four hundred and fifty—had been carved out and decorated or, as sometimes happened, replastered and repainted. After this, at various times, restoration would continue and, it is believed, about eleven new chapels were excavated.

It would be well before continuing this brief history of Ch'ien Fo Tung to describe more fully the chapels themselves. These artificial caves were hollowed—presumably by men working with picks and chisels—

12. Wei period wall painting: Cave 251 (P105), North wall. *See pages* 84, 85, 87
Buddha and bodhisattvas. Simulated beam-ends visible above Buddha's canopy. Two brackets made of wood have been inserted into wall at peak of ceiling and to the left, where this portion of the chapel adjoins the main portion. Oxidation is evident in darkness of skin and over-prominent highlights

15. Wei period sculpture: Cave 275 (P118/M). *See page* 91
Sculpture in high niche outside cave

into an almost sheer vertical cliff of conglomerate, a type of rock consisting of pebbles embedded in a comparatively soft matrix. This is apparently the material of the foothills of which the cliff is a part, but they are now covered, as is the cliff top, with sand piled to an immense height. The stream from the Nan Shan—South Mountains—has cut through the foothills to create a gravel-strewn valley, treeless and barren, which leads to the cliff.

Cut into the east face—the cliff is on a north-south axis—the chapels are ranged in irregular rows, one above the other, sometimes as high as a fourth or fifth level, for the distance of about one mile. The earliest chapels—those of the Six Dynasties period—are in the centre of the group; later dynasties seem to have followed a pattern of cutting their first chapels some distance from this central core, gradually approaching it with their later chapels, so that the newest of all are at the two extremities of this section of cliff.

The caves are more or less square in shape, and vary widely in size. Some are tremendous—measuring, according to an American scholar, twenty-seven feet high, seventy feet long and forty wide—and others are tiny rooms, which hold only one or two people. The majority of chapels fall between these two extremes, and in addition there are a number of individual shrines, merely niches containing one image or more, which are quite separate from the chapels.

Large or small, nearly all chapels have similarly shaped ceilings—like the hollow of a truncated pyramid, or, put another way, an inverted *tou*, the Chinese measure used for grains. It is believed that this shape was an adaptation, imposed by the nature of the conglomerate, of the 'lantern ceilings', a series of successively smaller squares laid cater-corner one above the other to form a roughly pyramidal shape, much used in Central Asia. Other ceilings, usually found in earlier chapels, are slanted to form an inverted wide-angle V, while at least one is gently rounded.

Cut into the same cliff but further north is another large group of caves, evidently the living-quarters of the monks who resided at the site. These are mostly undecorated, although wall-paintings—said to be in the Yüan dynasty style—have been found in one, and further search may reveal more.

Each of the cave-chapels has a single doorway which allows light and air to enter. This entrance is approached from a porch or ante-chapel, which may also lead to the porches of adjoining chapels. Some of these porches, forming an oblong passageway, were carved wholly from the cliff with one, or occasionally two, windows to admit light and to frame a view of the landscape outdoors. Others were cut partly from the cliff and partly constructed of timber and plaster. Several of these timbered structures, definitely dating to Sung and, it is claimed, even to the T'ang period, are still intact. It is possible that the whole façade of the cliff was at one time covered with them, for they would provide protection and entrance to every chapel in the complex. From outdoors, they would resemble a building, or perhaps a series of buildings, attached to the cliff. Many chapels at ground-level are directly reached through conventional temples of mud-brick and wood, but they are mostly of very recent date, as successive generations of restorers have apparently tried to keep them in good condition.

## Plastering, an Ancient Skill

Once hollowed out to form a room, the pebbly surface of the conglomerate was too rough to make immediately a flat bed for mural painting, and it was completely unsuitable for carving reliefs or sculptures. Plaster would, however, adhere to it tenaciously, and, when laid on thickly, formed an excellent and long-lasting surface on which to paint. It is obvious that the making of various types of plaster must have been a fine art here even before the first caves were excavated, for, after fifteen centuries, the wall-paintings of that time are still, to a great extent, firmly in place.

Mud from the river at the foot of the cliff seems to have been the base of this plaster, used both for walls and sculptures, presumably according to the correct formula for each. The plaster was usually mixed with dung and some fibrous material—animal hairs or straw or both—to give elasticity and cohesion.

The statues of Ch'ien Fo Tung include every size, from the colossal Buddha—built on a rock core—which is over ninety feet high, down to twelve-inch moulded Buddhas, simple little figures fastened to chapel walls in rows one above the other, forming a variation of the 'Thousand Buddha' wall design. Most of the smaller figures, half life-size or under, appear to have been cast from moulds, either wholly or in sections, while those which are life-size or greater, are modelled on wooden frames wrapped in straw.

In preparing the ceiling and walls of the chapels for decoration, the plaster was smoothed on in layers. After this, it was dressed with white kaolin—porcelain clay—or possibly powdered gypsum, and was then ready for the designs and colours to be applied.

No one knows exactly how this was done. Many

designs were obviously drawn free-hand, although other aids were also used, such as stencils, and compasses for the haloes. It is suspected that smaller designs were sometimes made with pounces—paper pricked out in designs which are transferred to the surface below when the 'pounce' is rubbed with coloured chalk or charcoal dust. One such pounce has been recovered from Ch'ien Fo Tung in recent years.

Although all these methods were probably used in decorating the thousands of square yards of wall surface at Ch'ien Fo Tung, they do not satisfactorily explain how the designs for the great paradise scenes of the T'ang period—immense harmonious compositions filled with multiple divinities, schematically grouped—were laid on the walls.

It is possible that these scenes—unbelievably intricate yet perfectly balanced and lucid—were copied from squared-off drawings on paper to proportionally larger squares on the wall surface. Yet this is hard to believe when one has seen the exquisite proportions of these paintings on walls and panels of different sizes. One feels, rather, that the walls themselves, the shape of the panel to be painted, the relationshio between these panels and other scenes to each other and to the chapel as a unit determined—in some manner—the method of applying the design.

A noted American authority has suggested that these patterns were geometrically plotted on the walls by means of strings—inked or chalked—that crossed from the opposite corners of the square or rectangle to be painted. The strings were then snapped against the white wall surface to form great diagonals. From the point at which the lines crossed were built up the series of triangles, chords and axes which determined the positions of the great central figure of the composition, his attendants, palaces, pavilions, musicians and dancers. Within this formal geometric pattern, fixing the proportions and relationships of the figures, the artists and artisans filled in the outlines and added the colour to conform to the Buddhist art canon, their own training and—often—their own genius.

Chemical analysts in the west have shown that the palette consisted in the ninth century and perhaps earlier of more than eleven pigments. From any shop which sells mineral specimens at least five of these can be bought: malachite (green), azurite (blue), orpiment (yellow), cinnabar (vermilion), iron oxide (earth red). Besides these, powdered and leaf gold and silver, lamp black, kaolin (white), red ochre, red and white lead—both of complicated manufacture—and some organic vegetable dyes were used. These and probably some other pigments, mixed with a glutinous material, were applied to the dry plaster. The wall-paintings, with one or two exceptions, are not painted in fresco technique, although they are often called frescoes for convenience and brevity. The sculptures, an integral part of the chapels, were painted with the same pigments as the murals.

In most cases, the construction of cave-chapels was commissioned and paid for by pious donors—of both sexes—whose portraits and often names were painted on the walls. Sometimes, it appears, the funds were subscribed by a great many presumably unrelated donors, judging from the numerous portraits in certain chapels, while in other cases, chapels seem to have been the gift of a few members of a wealthy family.

## The Shrine: Caves of Thousand Buddhas

To subscribe money for a chapel was an act of merit, through which the donor might hope to be reborn directly into paradise, escaping—either forever or for countless ages—rebirth in this world. Some donors have written this wish beside their portraits. Perhaps some of the many travellers who passed through Tun Huang used this method to implore protection for an impending journey or showed their gratitude for a safely completed—or profitable—one. Or, as happened elsewhere and in other religions, the donor may have fulfilled a vow.

However, performing a meritorious act is only part of the reason for ordering the construction and adornment of temples, for creating paintings and sculptures. These are only symbols which serve to render abstractions more easily understandable; they are 'aids' for the believer, and, by the truly devout, worshipped as such. For different people, according to the knowledge and faith of each, these symbols had different meanings and purposes.

The majestic paradises which are painted on the chapel walls and on banners were meant to inspire in the beholder faith in the blessings of heaven and the hope of sharing in them. This conception of heavens, of which Amitābha's Western Paradise was the most important, is a later development of Buddhism, since the Chinese, and certain other peoples, could not wholly accept the austere doctrines of early Buddhism. This taught that one could only escape rebirth through unceasing personal effort in many existences, and China turned to the more tender and comforting form, the Mahāyāna. Vastly complicated and containing many divergent beliefs, this system included the belief that the devout could hope—through good works or through meditation or the sheer power of faith, as well as other means—to avoid reincarnation and enter into heaven directly. In the popular belief, one could remain there, ecstatically happy, forever. In the Mahāyānist view, not only one's personal salvation was important but that of all creatures. This is indicated in the meaning of the name—the Great Vehicle—for by it many more souls were carried to salvation than by the Hīnayāna, or Lesser Vehicle. Within the Mahāyāna system, certain of the bodhisattvas assumed an importance equal to or greater than the Buddhas, of whom there were many. Through their infinite love for wretched, struggling humanity, the bodhisattvas elect to postpone the final bliss of Nirvāna, to which they are entitled, so that they may continue the unending labour of saving the souls of all, since 'all are destined, for Buddha-hood'.

The paradise scenes, then, were in one sense a visual and alluring illustration of the pleasures that awaited the blessed, but they were more besides. They demonstrate, also, one of the forms of existence a Buddha may have. In their first and highest form, the essence of all Buddhas is reality, the unchanging substance which is beyond earthly phenomena, for these are transient as 'the reflection of the moon on water'. In their second form, to aid the understanding of mankind, Buddhas may also appear incorporeally in splendour with their celestial courts. The third form, imperfect and distorted, when a Buddha dons the earthly shape of a human being, is assumed only out of boundless love, since this form is most easily comprehended by the mean intelligence of mankind. According to certain Buddhist sects, the devotee, through a difficult training and by acquiring special techniques, could learn to see radiant visions of the different paradises, the second form in which Buddhas may exist. Since the mystic of any country has the compulsion to translate his vision into a communicable form—whether it is in writing, painting or some other art—the paradise painting is for many the pious recording of a vision, interpreted, it may be, by others.

Because in China, Indian and Central Asian art met a tradition equally powerful, original and, though very different, extremely advanced, it was inevitable that Chinese artists should absorb the foreign elements of their religious art, fuse them into a style and impose on them a conception that was peculiarly Chinese. This process had been completed by the T'ang dynasty, whose models were considered so perfect by subsequent generations that they would not or could not substantially change them even to the present day.

The shape and form of the Buddhist divinities, which had been evolved in India and Gandhāra and which had largely filtered to China through Central Asia, retained to a great degree their 'foreign' appearance, although even this was subtly changed by Chinese artists. The faces of the deities became more Chinese, the body and pose lose their sensuous Indian lines and soft tenderness to become more symmetrical and decorous. In keeping partly with Chinese ideas of propriety, the figures are more fully clothed. Following the art canon of this period, recurrent in Chinese history, personal and individual characteristics, including those of sex, are subordinated to show an ideal, a generic type. This can be seen as well in the paintings of secular subjects at

14. Wei period, sculpture and wall painting: Cave 254 (P105), South wall.
*See pages* 84, 85, 87

Scenes from Buddha's last birth (?) and *jātaka* tale. Central panel represents assault by Mara and other events of Buddha's life (?). Panel at right is *jātaka* of the tigress, whose hindquarters can be seen at extreme lower right. Two niches contain painted clay sculptures; the one at right is badly defaced. Demons on dado

15. Wei period: Cave 254 (P105), South wall and ceiling. *See pages* 84, 87, 91
Detail of sculptured figure in niche, unrestored. Wooden brackets at peak of ceiling barely visible at top centre, as ceiling and east wall of this chapel have been blackened with soot from refugees' cook-fires.

Ch'ien Fo Tung, although fairly detailed portraiture was obviously appreciated also.

In making the paintings and sculptures of the Buddhas, bodhisattvas and attendants, whether grouped in their heavens or not, the Chinese artists used a style that is formal and idealized, in keeping with their divine subjects. When they turned to secular scenes, usually painted at the side, below or even within the panels allotted the divinities, artists worked in the contemporary secular style—free, vivid, naturalistic.

The human actors of these side-scenes, which illustrate stories from the scriptures, admonitions to laymen and sometimes historical events, are charmingly drawn in the dress of their period, using the objects of their daily life. This technique—a formal rendering for sacred subjects, following traditional iconography; a natural, contemporary style for the secular—is common, of course, in much religious art throughout the world. Even now, one sees it in the little lithographs given Sunday school children in America. Christ is always drawn with the long hair, beard and robes prescribed by tradition, while the children at His knee wear the clothes of to-day.

Following another frequently-used convention of religious art, the figures of the side-scenes—monks and nuns, lords and ladies, knights on horseback, cowherds and grooms—are all drawn on a far smaller scale than the main divinities. The serene grandeur and majesty of the holy ones is enhanced by the littleness and liveliness of the tiny figures at their feet who pray, plough, fight in battles, weep, go on pilgrimages. By sheer contrast the earth-dwellers are reduced to size, a busy group of ants, unceasingly active before the wisdom-filled calm of the gods. It is apparent that the artists of Ch'ien Fo Tung knew the effects they wished to achieve and suited to this their designs, proportions, colours and style, both in their paintings and sculptures.

The portraits of donors—both the large, detailed figures and the smaller, drawn in a few lines—are in the secular style also, and are often an important guide to the placing of an undated cave. Fashions, then as now, changed, and it is often known from other sources what was the particular hat, the headdress, the gown of a certain period.

If fashions were fickle, it appears that the devotion accorded Ch'ien Fo Tung remained more or less constant during its first thousand years of existence. That Tun Huang lost its position and importance astride the main trade-routes, thus adversely affecting Ch'ien Fo Tung, was due to previous and continuing far-reaching events in Inner Asia, Europe and elsewhere.

Even before Tun Huang had fallen to the Tangguts, the Turkish tribes, gradually becoming Mohammedans, had from the seventh century swept down wave on wave southward into Central Asia. The history of the oasis-kingdoms there became a scarlet tapestry woven with the threads of invasion and warfare, pillage and conquest, which in time destroyed their finely-wrought culture, blended from so many sources.

By the fifteenth century, the final remnants of Buddhism had vanished there. The language of the Central Asian oases would remain Turkish, their religion Islam until the present day. This militant faith would extend its hold even into western China and elsewhere, and today Tun Huang's province of Kansu is politically dominated by the Chinese Muslims—unless the Chinese communists have altered matters.

In the thirteenth century, the great Mongol invasions under Genghis Khan and his sons engulfed the lands from China to eastern Europe. Although this great empire, largest in history, broke up rapidly, one of its most solid segments—China—became the domain of Genghis's grandson, Kublai. The lamaist form of Buddhism, still embraced by the Mongols and Tibetans, showed itself in the cave-chapels of Ch'ien Fo Tung painted at this time. Marco Polo, Venetian official of Kublai, visited Tun Huang, then called Sha Chow—'The City of Sands'—and describes with obvious distaste the 'idolatrous customs' of its people, perhaps basing his opinion on their peculiar attachment to the Thousand Buddha Caves.

In the fourteenth century, the Yüan dynasty of the Mongols in China was replaced after much bloodshed by a native Chinese dynasty, the Ming. The western boundaries and influence of the Ming did not extend much beyond the end of the Great Wall at Chia Yü Kuan, nearly two hundred miles east of Tun Huang. The history of Ch'ien Fo Tung becomes rather obscure at this time, although the Imperial Geography of the Ch'ing Dynasty informs us that for the first seventy years of Ming rule, Tun Huang was under Chinese administration, which was then abolished. A modern account says that 'Tun Huang was given away to the barbarians and became their pasture'. Presumably the fertile oasis came under Mongol tribes. If they were lamaists, we may assume they took some interest in Ch'ien Fo Tung and perhaps in making restorations. So far, however, there seems to be no evidence of either new caves having been excavated or old ones repaired or repainted at this time.

During the Ming dynasty, a thriving sea-trade carried by Arab, Indian and Chinese ships had developed, thus removing what might have been a strong pressure to reopen the overland routes on the west. Gradually China's eastern coast became her front-gate, or rather, her ports a series of gates. They were to remain so until the mid-twentieth century. While the Ming were on the throne, Europe began to reach out for the trade of China and the Indies. Columbus sailed west, crossing the uncharted Atlantic in hopes of discovering a new route to the fabulous lands described by Marco Polo, and unintentionally intercepted the continents of America, with fateful consequences.

Tun Huang, like the other oasis-cities of Kansu, became a distant military outpost under the Manchus, alien rulers of China from the mid-seventeenth century. Their armies surged, as had those of T'ang before them, into Central Asia. Here they broke, once for all, the power of a great Mongol confederation which had threatened them for over a century. The oasis-cities of eastern Central Asia also became garrisons, largely but not always, under Chinese administration. This area was called Sinkiang—'The New Dominion'—and later was incorporated as a province of China.

Ch'ien Fo Tung probably enjoyed a mild renascence during the height of Manchu power. Tun Huang was then part of the chain of defence which extended from Kashgar in western Sinkiang to the Yellow River. The Manchu emperors, especially the famous Ch'ien Lung, settled many immigrants on the Tun Huang oasis, where apparently the population had greatly dwindled.

16. Wei period wall painting: Cave 254 (P105). *See pages* 84, 85, 86
Buddha reincarnated as King of the Sibis (?). Small figure, lower right, saws at Buddha's left leg; white bird (dove?) hovers at upper right

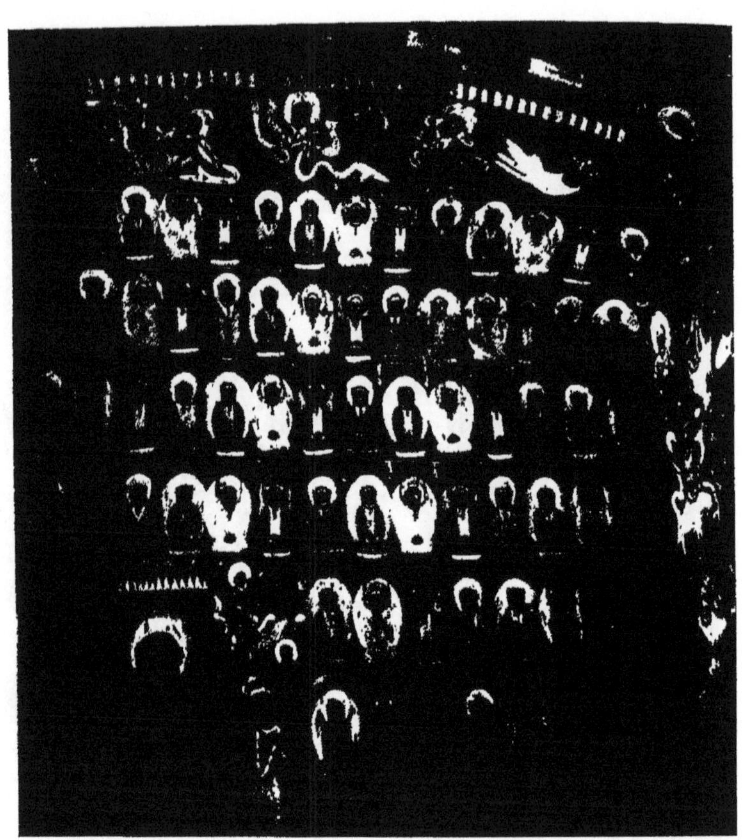

17. Wei period wall painting: Cave 272 (P188/J), South wall. *See pages* 84, 85
Buddha, 'Thousand Buddhas' design, *apsara*, simulated beams. Portion of west wall (*see frontispiece*) visible at right. Ceiling is gently curved, its central design a 'lantern' square

These immigrants were mostly from other parts of Kansu and each group may have moved from its native place *en bloc*, for each section of the large Tun Huang oasis is named for a prefecture of Kansu, reproducing in miniature a map of the province. Monks, although probably not many, were in residence at Ch'ien Fo Tung. By the mid-nineteenth century, however, the Manchu power began to disintegrate, especially in the western provinces, and the cave-chapels fell into neglect.

In Europe, great excitement was caused—in interested circles—by archaeological finds in Central Asia, which appeared to be the remains of the 'lost Buddhist civilization'. British, French, German, Russian and Japanese archaeological missions began a brisk competition to bring home manuscripts, paintings, sculptures and wall-fragments for western scholarship. The greatest of these scholar-explorers was the British archaeologist, Sir Aurel Stein, of whom we shall hear more.

Towards the turn of the century, Ch'ien Fo Tung found a curious would-be saviour. This was a simple Taoist monk named Wang Yuan-lu of Hupeh province in central China. He had come upon the deserted caves during a journey and, moved by the neglect he saw, dedicated his life to restoring the site. Penniless himself, he made long begging trips to acquire the money for this pious task. With the funds thus gained, Wang diverted the stream to create a small oasis at the foot of the cliff, planted poplar trees and built a guest-house for pilgrims. He began or continued construction of a building to cover the massive statue of Buddha,—then open to the elements—and devoted much effort to restoring chapels. His ambitions for his beloved oasis were great and he was often short of funds.

 V.S.O.

During the repair of a large chapel in 1899, he found by chance that part of one frescoed wall was hollow. Tearing it out, he discovered a small room packed, floor to ceiling, with manuscripts and paintings, obviously very old. This was, although Wang did not know it, the library of the monastic community—or a large part of it—which had been sealed up in the eleventh century and forgotten.

Sir Aurel Stein, continuing his fruitful exploration of Central Asia, reached Tun Huang in 1907. His aim was to visit the caves, of which he had heard glowing reports from a distinguished Hungarian geologist, Professor de Lóczy, who had visited the site in 1879. While at Tun Huang, Sir Aurel heard rumours of the manuscripts which, when he had seen them, proved to be even more valuable and interesting than he had dared hope. There then remained the task of acquiring them from the reluctant Wang, and in this, so Sir Aurel says, he was aided by the spirit of the ancient pilgrim, Hsüan Tsang, patron saint of both himself and the Taoist monk. When among the first manuscripts examined by Stein there appeared rolls carried from India and translated by Hsüan Tsang, Wang felt this good omen permitted him to trust his guest. By tact and diplomacy, Sir Aurel acquired twenty-nine cases of manuscripts, paintings, embroideries and other objects, and Wang, with evident joy, received a large donation of silver to continue the pious project of restoring Ch'ien Fo Tung. Many gaudily painted new statues and brightly redecorated walls as well as the soaring roofs of the building to cover the colossal Buddha are mute evidence that the good monk applied himself single-heartedly to his chosen task.

## The 'Sealed Library'

The paintings and book-rolls which Sir Aurel shipped from Ch'ien Fo Tung were of incalculable value to western—and world—scholarship. Included in the find was the first block-printed book of which there is any record, dated the equivalent of A.D. 868. There were many Buddhist scriptures and commentaries in Chinese—some previously lost—as well as accounts of local secular history. Manuscripts in hitherto little-known Central Asian languages and in Sanskrit and Tibetan revealed much concerning this region and of other religions which had flourished there. The textile fragments, ex-votos and a larger number of paintings on silk and paper cast new light on the art of the T'ang dynasty. Incompletely described here, the contents of the sealed chapel were one of the most important archaeological finds ever made.

A year later, a noted French savant, Professor Paul Pelliot, headed an expedition to Ch'ien Fo Tung and obtained a good portion of such manuscripts, block-printed rolls and paintings as were left. Under most difficult conditions Professor Pelliot's mission made a large collection of photographs of the chapel interiors, the most extensive so far published. These form the principal basis for western study of the art of Ch'ien Fo Tung.

The Chinese government, a struggling republic from 1911 and, at the time, weak and ineffectual, soon after this ordered the remainder of the contents of the 'hidden manuscript-chapel' to be sent to the capital, then at Peking. Apart from a 'nest-egg' prudently laid aside by Wang and part of which was acquired by Stein during a later visit, many manuscripts were plundered by officials and handlers on the journey to

Peking. Gossip has it that an unspecified number of books and paintings are cached away in certain—also unspecified—houses in Tun Huang.

'Tun Huang paintings' turn up with fair regularity in the curio shops of China. It is usual for connoisseurs to describe these variously as 'a Ming copy of a T'ang painting'—this was the verdict on one purchased by the writer—as a 'fake' and so on.

Even distant ripples from the maelstrom of the first World War reached Ch'ien Fo Tung. About 1920, a band of Russian refugees, fleeing the Bolshevik revolution, found asylum for several months in the caves. They left a permanent souvenir of their visit: a number of painted walls blackened by soot from cook-fires and improvised sleeping platforms, names in Russian script, and drawings—of that type which shows a man with a cigar in his mouth—scratched on the soft frescoed plaster.

A few years after this, Professor Langdon Warner of Harvard University visited Ch'ien Fo Tung and secured a wall fragment and sculpture, which have enabled the chemical analyses to be made concerning the T'ang pigments and painting materials.

Abbot Wang died in 1931, and some of his successors tried to carry on his work. They had not, on the whole, his zeal. Furthermore Kansu had been for some time rent with civil wars, making such projects difficult. If the immediate local situation was quiet in the fourth month, usually our May, Ch'ien Fo Tung's annual festival was held. Hundreds of people came from the surrounding areas for the three-day celebration. During the rest of the year, Ch'ien Fo Tung resumed its air of almost complete desolation, which the two or three

18. Wei period wall painting: Chapel 455 (P124), North wall.
*See pages* 69, 84, 85
Detail of large Buddha with attendant bodhisattva

19. Wei period, wall painting: Cave 288 (P120/P). *See page* 87
Ceiling showing four frequently-used ceiling designs: from top to bottom: lotus medallions, lotus bud and pod, 'lantern roof', 'Thousand Buddhas'

monks at the site would not or could not remedy, either through indifference or lack of funds.

In the late thirties, during the Sino-Japanese war, the Chinese government sent surveyors and engineers to Kansu. With *corvée* labour drawn from the countryside, they turned the ancient road through the Kansu corridor into a motor highway, so that war materials could be hauled down by truck from Russia. Ch'ien Fo Tung's bad luck began, to quote a Chinese account, for the shrine became accessible to a horde of casual sightseers and, bluntly expressed, vandals. Except for the collapse of much of the cliff face—an unavoidable disaster occurring during the course of many decades, which had damaged many chapels—more destruction was probably caused to the wall-paintings and sculptures of Ch'ien Fo Tung during the first few years of the motor road than at any comparable period of the caves' centuries-old history.

In 1943, in the midst of the second World War, the Chinese government, then taking refuge in Chungking, set up the National Art Research Institute of Tun Huang, which was to have custody of the site. This was done in response to the 'petitions of art lovers', a movement spearheaded by a few public-spirited Chinese scholars and artists. The work of the conscientious group attached to the Tun Huang Institute will be described in the next section.

Officially declaring Ch'ien Fo Tung of 'archaeological and historic' importance and extending over it official protection is symbolic perhaps of the profound transformation taking place in every phase of Chinese life. This transformation,—in reality, a revolution which has been going on for many years—is painful and often violent. It is so deep and far-reaching that, say, the China of the year 1910 will seem closer to the eras of Han, the Six Dynasties, and T'ang to name a few, than to the China of a generation hence.

The continuity of Chinese culture, unbroken for centuries although it changed and developed greatly within itself, faces—and has faced for several decades—its most serious challenge in the impact of western technology and beliefs, of which communism is the latest to gain power.

In this process, ancient landmarks, once a vital part of the culture, become objects of scholarly interest or are used for new, 'practical' purposes: the not recent practice of turning temples into schools is a striking example of the increasing secularization of Chinese life. Ancient ideals and customs either recede quietly or are violently hurled out of the mainstream of rapidly changing daily life and become memories—venerated, hated or merely ignored. So Ch'ien Fo Tung, although continuing a shrine, is primarily regarded as an archaeological monument by China's two most recent governments, those of the Kuo Min Tang and the Communists.

Another chapter for Ch'ien Fo Tung began in the fall of 1949, when the Chinese communist armies took over the whole of Kansu province. Sinkiang, the former 'Serindia', fell a little later.

It is an odd turn of history that the most recent events—the rise to power of the Chinese communists and their alliance with Soviet Russia—may revive the past importance of this area where the two share a common border.

Kansu may again become a front-gate to China, a

gate which we hope will be open, in a happier day than ours, to all. But Ch'ien Fo Tung, until it has vanished utterly, will remain a sacred oasis—if only in memory—both for Buddhists and for those of all nations and religions who care for works of beauty made by the hand of man.

20. Wei period sculpture: Cave 259 (P111), North wall. *See page* 91
Seated Buddha in niche, extreme right of three such figures

21. Western Wei wall painting: Cave 285 (P120/N), Ceiling. *See page* 88
*Apsara*, demons, mythical beasts. Rope ending in bell-shaped 'tassels' lower centre. Ceiling edge visible lower left

22. Western Wei: Cave 285 (P120/N), West wall, south (left). *See page* 88.
Side of main alcove. Wall-painting in the Central Asian style

25. Western Wei wall painting: Cave 285 (P120/N), North wall, east (right) side, and portion of ceiling. *See pages* 88, 89

Buddhas and attendants, donors, upper portions of two alcoves. Ceiling curve may be seen by comparing row of Buddhas at right with those in centre of picture

# PART TWO

# Westward Journey to the Sacred Oasis

## CHAPTER IV

# Search for a Mechanized Camel

In his secret heart almost everyone carries the name of some place on earth which he hopes to see before he dies, whether it is a palm-lined Pacific island, the pyramids of Egypt, or India's Taj Mahal.

In 1939 I had chosen mine—the Thousand Buddha Caves of Tun Huang. The summer school of the University of Michigan offered that year an excellent course in Chinese art. I had spent three months at this heady banquet, where four thousand years of painting, ceramics, bronzes, frescoes and sculptures—besides such hors d'œuvres as jades, ivories and cloisonné—were laid before us, served up in photographs, lantern slides and lectures. After this hastily devoured—almost indigestible—feast, the memory of the Thousand Buddha Caves had remained to haunt and tantalize me. I never really expected to see them with my own eyes, however. The only westerners who had this good fortune seemed to be eminent scholars, under the wing of important organizations, who spent weeks travelling there in horse-carts, sacks of bullion concealed in their luggage.

## Search for a Mechanized Camel

Yet exactly nine years later, in the summer of 1948, I found myself in Lanchow, capital of Kansu province, looking for ways and means to reach Tun Huang, westward along the Silk Route which led out of Lanchow. The Chinese portion of the Silk Route was now prosaically called the Northwest Highway; across its vast and tortuous length lumbered trucks as well as ever-dwindling caravans of camels and horses. During the second World War, Russian trucks had carried guns, grenades and munitions from the Siberian railhead, through Sinkiang and the Kansu corridor, to be unloaded at Lanchow for shipment to Chungking and elsewhere. But by 1948 all that remained of this *rapprochement* was a portrait of Stalin, which someone had forgotten to remove, in Lanchow's principal hotel.

It had taken me only six hours to reach Lanchow from Peking, flying over the Gobi desert which, from the air, looks like an immense buff-coloured bedspread spattered with brown oak leaves, the finger-like pattern etched by eroded gullies. Tun Huang was closer to Lanchow than was Peking, being a little over five hundred and fifty miles as the crow—or airplane—flies. No airplanes, or crows, carried passengers to Tun Huang however, and I was not sorry for I had hoped, secretly, to travel by horse or camel, surely the most fitting way to venture on the Silk Route.

My Lanchow friends, a little surprised at this sentimentality, told me that the camels were out to grass, and that the trip by horse would take two months—the earth-bound road was over eight hundred miles—and Allah alone knew how long to arrange. I was short of time. They advised me to travel by truck—if I could find one bound for Tun Huang—but urged me

24. Western Wei wall painting: Cave 285 (P120/N), North wall, west (left) portion. *See pages* 88, 89

Detail of group similar to those in plate 22. Small seated Buddhas on ceiling edge are surrounded by deer, trees; one is flanked by a tiger. Man shooting yak at upper right

25. Sui period sculpture: Cave 285 (120/J), West wall. *See page* 91
Buddha and two arhats. Believed largely unrestored

not to be disappointed if I never reached the caves at all. Why not, they asked, go to the famous monastery of Kumbum, only two days away, for which trucks departed daily? I felt this could come later, and we began to look for Tun Huang trucks.

During the first few days, I did not worry much about my transportation, for Lanchow is a fascinating frontier city—a point of departure for Turkestan, Tibet and Mongolia—as different from the charming sophistication of Peking as a lump of coal from a jade necklace.

On Lanchow's dusty, beaten-earth roads, cotton-clad muleteers drove their animals past booted Mongol horsemen and elegantly dressed Chinese from the coastal cities. Turki merchants from Sinkiang, wearing gaily embroidered caps and black corduroy suits, sold rugs and felt from Khotan, the raisins and dried melons of Turfan and Hami. A family of white Russians, émigrés who had drifted here after the Bolshevik revolution, ran a confectioner's shop where you could buy cream-covered cakes and hot tea in tall glasses, while less fortunate compatriots carried long brooms and stood dismally at the centre of town waiting for jobs white-washing the walls of mud-brick houses.

In the north of Lanchow, near the iron bridge which spans the turbulent Yellow River, was a street devoted to the needs of caravans—saddles, bridles, red-dyed yak tails to adorn the lead animal. Conspicuous in the city were the Chinese Muslims—the men in black gowns and white skull caps, the women gaily dressed and wearing half-veils—for somewhat over half of Lanchow's population is of this faith, a slightly higher average, it is believed, than for the province as a whole.

## Search for a Mechanized Camel

One pastime united us all at this time of the year—eating the melons, sold at every street corner, for which Kansu and Sinkiang are famous. Their incredible succulence and sweetness are due to 'the earth and water' here, the local people say. The older ones add that, since the passing of the empire, melons have deteriorated sadly, because the melon-growers have no incentive to produce their finest fruits for the imperial tribute. I could not believe this. The insipid California honeydew, for instance, whose seeds were sent to Kansu by an American war-time vice-president, was here rechristened the 'Wallace melon' in his honour. The result was rather like a transplanted daisy turning into an orchid.

Even the delectable melons were small consolation after calling daily at numerous truck-owning organizations—including the Army, the Highway Administration, the Post Office and even one notorious smuggler—to be told that they *never* ran trucks to Tun Huang. That oasis, each explained patiently, was eighty miles off the Northwest Highway, on the abandoned route which had formerly crossed southern Sinkiang. Perhaps I could reach Ansi, the nearest city on the main highway, but—forestalling my inevitable plea for a ride—not aboard one of their trucks, which were booked for weeks ahead. From Ansi to Tun Huang—? they shrugged and shook their heads. They did not know how I was to manage it, but, to spare my feelings, said they thought occasional trucks made the trip.

Travel has never been easy in the northwest, and the motto of the Highway Administration, which maintains the road, was 'Communications come first!', painted on a thousand earth walls. Ten times more travellers—merchants, officials, soldiers, pilgrims and ordinary people, *lao pai hsing*—applied for places on trucks than could ever be carried. I relived sympathetically the anguish of ancient travellers who had tried, in vain, to attach themselves to each westbound caravan.

I had the illusion at times that the truck had become domesticated here, a motorized camel of whims and fancies which had insinuated itself into the ancient pattern of desert transportation. Yet I knew it was not so. The 'motorized camel', bearing with it new values and a host of machine-minded men, was destroying the quiet and dignity of the desert, a process that would be completed when the desert was knit with the iron bands of railroads and the invisible paths of airplanes, the air above black with the smoke of factory chimneys.

In the end, my Lanchow friends, who had tried tirelessly to find transportation for me, agreed reluctantly—for they felt this to be a breach of etiquette towards a guest—that I should take *any* truck as far as it would go and then see what would happen.

One chilly dawn, I climbed aboard a dilapidated vehicle which belonged to the government-owned Oil Company. It was bound for Chiu Ch'uan, the former Hsü Chow, more than halfway to Tun Huang. Near Chiu Ch'uan were the company's oil fields, site of the only operating oil wells in China. This truck had hauled gasolene, refined at the fields, to Lanchow and was to return with the equally precious empty drums.

I sat in the cab of the truck between the driver and the mechanic, the seat of honour and comfort which belonged by rights to an army officer travelling with us. I knew that this place was reserved for officials, army officers or women carrying babies, but the officer insisted that, as a stranger in Kansu, I take it. To silence my protests, he gallantly joined the other passengers on the gasolene drums piled high at the back of the truck.

With an earsplitting crash of gears we started off, crossed the iron bridge, and turned west along the road cut into the river bank. The Yellow River, truthfully and tritely called 'China's Sorrow', is indeed yellow, heavy with the earth it tears from its banks in a headlong rush to the sea. The only craft we saw were rafts made of inflated goatskins tied to a bamboo frame, so light that the hardy navigator, after a swift ride downstream, could carry it home—at leisure—on his shoulders. Along the river banks were immense wooden water wheels—some, over eighty feet in diameter—which sent water pulsing along pipes of split logs to the wheat and millet fields and orchards which lined the road.

We soon stopped for the most important business of a truck-driver's day—collecting 'yellow fish'. Completely non-aquatic, these are travellers—the Kansu version of a hitch-hiker—who, lacking the necessary influence to purchase a legal ticket from a truck-owning organization, make their arrangements directly with the truck-driver, after much haggling. Since 'yellow fish' contribute most of the driver's income, unless he is reckless enough to carry contraband such as gold, he cheerfully bears the inconvenience and delays they cause. Even the legitimate passengers do not complain—although the term 'yellow fish' is derived from a fish that is closely packed like sardines elsewhere—since they never know when they may be yellow fish themselves. The driver must allow these illegal passengers to disembark before passing customs at each

26. Sui period wall painting: Cave 390 (P150), North wall. *See page* 91
Buddhas and attendants, donors, simulated beam-ends, surmounted by *apsara*.
Cartouches, in which donors' names are written, are found beneath donors, some of whom are attended by servants.

27. T'ang period wall painting. Cave 217 (P70), West wall, ceiling of alcove
*See page* 93

Buddha and attendant bodhisattvas. Two groups of donors worship smaller Buddha at upper right; cartouche below Buddha contains no names

city, and must later pick them up at a pre-arranged point outside the city walls. I wondered if the traveller of long ago, unable to persuade a caravan-owner to include him in the caravan, had sometimes had better success dealing with the chief camel-driver.

The first night we spent, not at one of the large oasis-cities where we would find special truck-hostels, originally built to accommodate Russian drivers during the war, but at a road-side caravanserai which had a well. Our truck had broken down several times during the day and, with the yellow fish delays, we had not been able to reach Wu Wei, once called Liang Chow, and the first important city out of Lanchow.

We stopped here because our driver was unwilling to travel at night from fear of bandits and *kwei*—spirits—although he said no trucks had been robbed for several years. In any case, the headlights were broken.

The rheumy-eyed venerable lady of this desolate establishment, which seemed to exemplify the passing of the desert's old ways, cooked supper for us on a little mud stove fed with twigs and dung, fanned to a high heat by wooden bellows. Some caravan-drivers, also staying here, inspected our truck critically, and I went into the courtyard we shared with their mules and horses, tied up for the night with their wooden saddles and loads—grain in camels' hair bags—lying on the ground beside them. Later in the truck-hostels, the courtyard would be occupied by trucks, all as anxiously tended by their mechanics as these muleteers had fed and watered their animals.

Wu Wei, a walled city set amid the cultivated fields and fortified farm-houses of a large semi-oasis, was a drab, undistinguished model of a fairly prosperous desert city, one of several we saw. Once a thriving market-town, from which large caravans departed for Peking, it retained a certain importance from being the first truck-stop out of Lanchow and the junction of a motor road running through Mongol territory to Peking.

The former carved gates and up-turned roof ends of the houses and shops on its principal street had been replaced by smooth false fronts of stucco, which seemed to make one continuous gray building pierced with arched doorways. This 'modernization', of which the townsfolk were very proud, was enhanced in another city by a public address system installed in the Drum Tower, situated as tradition decrees where the principal north-south street intersects the east-west street in the centre of town.

Outside of Wu Wei, the green fields thinned out to stony desert lightly covered with grey-green scrub. During one 'tea' or 'car-repairing' halt—the terms were interchangeable—I noticed workmen repairing the road with mud-bricks that looked rather old. The foreman, a northerner and the only one who could understand me, said that they were taking the bricks from a *ku ch'eng*—ancient city—a few *li* away. When I asked how old the city was, he said it had been built in Han times. The bricks were, then, about two thousand years old.

We had taken two days to cover what the mail truck—best and most lightly loaded on the road—travelled in one. This was to be our time-ratio for the entire trip to Chiu Ch'uan. Our truck was old; we stopped frequently to overhaul it and to drink tea from enormous Shanghai-made thermos bottles carried by the seasoned travellers of our party. During these halts, it was the custom of the road, a continuation of the warm hospitality once traditional in the desert, that each person share with fellow-passengers whatever food or drink he carried. With this periodic redistribution of our combined supplies of melons, tea or *mo-mo*, the delicious local bread, each halt evolved into a picnic.

This was the rainy season—August—and twice we spent the night at a caravanserai beside a river, swollen by a few hours of rain from a stream to a torrent, too deep and swift for our truck to ford. It seemed strange that rain should ever fall on this desert, so inhospitable between oases and their rivers, yet before we reached Chiu Ch'uan it had rained each day and several cities were ankle-deep in mud.

From the time we left Lanchow, we had more or less followed the Great Wall, that same wall I had once seen at Nan K'ou, not far from Peking. Sometimes it was a mere snake-like mound rising from the desert with ridges scalloped by wind, sand and time; elsewhere it was almost full height. A short distance from the wall we occasionally passed the watch-towers which had been part of the Great Wall defence system. Before each crenellated tower, square in shape, stood five smaller structures in which the beacon fires had been lit to signal the next tower in the chain. Messages of approaching invaders, thus relayed, could rapidly reach the nearest garrison. Now weeds grew between the earthen bricks of the towers, and slogans painted on the sides urged the reader to 'strike down the communist bandits'. There seemed to be in the northwest a passion for writing on walls exhortations which ran from bidding all join in the post-war reconstruction of the country to not forgetting the daily brushing of teeth.

Occasionally we passed the city walls, eroded by wind and sand, of what must have once been flourishing communities. Wars had devastated the populations, most recently during the Mohammedan rebellions of the past century; lack of trade had ruined their livelihood. The desert had smothered the once cultivated fields and choked up the wells. Now, through holes in the crumbling battlements one could see sometimes a little encampment of perhaps half a dozen people or no one at all. Other cities, more fortunate, managed to retain a remnant of their people and fields, yet, falling between the regular truck stops, they seemed to eke out their existence in a miasma of weary, poverty-stricken decay.

On our third day, I visited one such city—Shantan, which lies between Wu Wei and the large rice-producing oasis of Kan Chow, or Chang Yeh. During the war, the Baillie School of the Chinese Industrial Co-operative Movement had been moved here from an area threatened by the Japanese. This school, then financed largely by British and American funds, trains young Chinese girls and boys, many of them orphans or otherwise destitute, so that they may return to organize and run small industries in the villages of rural China. A larger aim of the school, as of the Movement, was to bring the industrial revolution to China in a way which would most help and least dislocate the thousands of villages of which China is composed. Our driver had said, most agreeably, that he would wait two hours outside the city walls while I ran in to see friends who had moved with the school.

28. T'ang period wall painting: Cave 217 (P70), West wall, north (right) portion of alcove. *See page* 95

Arhats, Bodhisattvas, Haloes and Clouds. Background to sculptural elements now lost

29. T'ang period wall painting: Cave 217 (P70), West wall, panel at north (right) of alcove. *See page* 94

Bodhisattva. Alcove containing new image is at left

## Workshops and a Stupa

The busy workshops of the school where bricks, glass, rugs, paper and many other things were made, presented a curious contrast to the crumbling beauty of the town, too poor and unimportant to have suffered 'modernization'. Walking down the wide main streets, lined with poplars, I could easily imagine how lovely other Kansu oasis-cities had once been.

The gateways of the buildings, set in earth-brick walls, were charmingly carved and painted. Graceful wooden archways, now named for eminent political personages, spanned the roads. Every third or fourth building seemed to be a temple, its pretty courtyard visible through the gate. I heard later that Shantan, whose population had dwindled nowadays to an estimated three thousand, contained over two hundred and fifty temples, not counting the Mohammedan mosques. Opposite the temples were small open-air theatres where townspeople or itinerant actors performed plays during festivals. The people, apathetically going about their daily tasks, seemed intensely poor and disease-ridden.

Dominating the city and visible for miles was a tremendous domed stupa of mud-brick and plaster, Fa T'a Sse, said to contain a Hair of King Ashoka, the great Buddhist king of India. The noble lines of this tower, a hemisphere set on a great square base, heightened the faded and mellow charm of the city.

Chatting hastily with friends, admiring the many enterprises of the school which extended from irrigation and coal-mining projects to weaving rugs—a foremost handcraft of the north-west—from Tun Huang fresco designs, visiting a few streets of the city I regretted bitterly that my stay would be only two hours instead of two years. For Shantan and its environs mirrored millennia of Chinese border history.

A neolithic site had been uncovered during excavations for the irrigation project, yielding among other things pots with a curious raised design, unlike any others so far discovered. In the small courtyard of a temple was a Nestorian Christian baptismal font made of stone, a relic perhaps from the days when colonies of this heretical sect were scattered through Central Asia and China. Another temple was decorated with T'ang frescoes, which local scholars considered as fine as the best at Ch'ien Fo Tung. Near the school, tottering but still erect, was a house continuously owned by the same family since the eleventh century. The two-story dwelling had been left untouched since it was cursed, I was told, during the Sung dynasty, when an irate Taoist abbot declared: the house 'would never be sold and never be repaired'.

Glancing at my watch, I hurried back to the truck and was politely scolded for running hard at this altitude—approximately six thousand feet above sea level.

On the seventh day, within sight of our destination of Chiu Ch'uan, the way was barred by the river which had risen several feet across the road during the night's rain. An enterprising owner of a type of horse-drawn cart much used in the north west—consisting of a wooden platform mounted on the axle of two wheels taller than a man—was 'ferrying' people across the river for a certain sum. The passengers and driver of our truck, after a hasty conference, decided that, of them all, the army officer could offer me the best accommodation in Chiu Ch'uan. Assuring me that his wife would be delighted if I stayed with them 'indefinitely', we and several others bargained with the cart-owner to take us in to the city.

I was amazed—though perhaps I should not have been—to discover at Chiu Ch'uan that the Highway Administration ran a passenger-carrying truck to Tun Huang twice a month. Furthermore, I would only have to wait five days until its next scheduled trip. I was as delighted as if I had been told in America that my bus would leave in fifteen minutes. I realized then that I had slipped imperceptibly into the leisurely pace of the desert, where time no longer mattered.

During this five-day interval, I encountered by chance an American girl, travelling in the opposite direction, and we both received permission to visit the oil wells, some seventy miles distant from Chiu Ch'uan. Lao Chün Miao, the name of this site, was a fascinating mixture of ancient and modern. Set on a barren hill-side almost without vegetation, to which all food had to be carried, was the complete paraphernalia of a Texas oil field, with some piquant Kansu additions, such as a herd of camels used to haul coal—found near here in abundance—for the refinery. We witnessed at two in the morning the exciting bustle of 'bringing in' a well, as the workmen cheered. These were part of the three thousand local men employed here, the officials and engineers of the company, like almost all skilled or trained personnel in Kansu, coming from other provinces. Although the workmen had had no previous experience with machinery more complicated than a spinning wheel, their performance was excellent, according to an American engineer stationed at Lao Chün Miao.

The plentiful oil seepage of this place is said to have

greased the cart wheels of Genghis Khan, a figure very much alive in the memory of the north-west. His tomb is some sixty miles from Lanchow and in undisturbed years a great ceremony is held in Mongolia on the anniversary of his death.

During the war with Japan, modern machinery was painfully shipped to the field by truck, camel, horse and on the backs of men, so that a local source of gasolene might be available to the Chinese government, then virtually cut off from supplies abroad. The Chiu Ch'uan wells now supplied lubricating oil and gasolene for the trucks of the north-west, and some was exported to neighbouring provinces.

In Chiu Ch'uan, I visited a temple where, as at Kanchow, there was a plaster 'reclining Buddha' close on a hundred feet long, considered one of the sights of the city. The priest who showed me through the temple was delighted to hear that I was on my way to the sacred Thousand Buddha Caves. Because of this pious journey, he pressed on me a touching—and most welcome—gift of eggs, hardboiled in tea.

Early one morning, I boarded the 'regular car' to Tun Huang, a former Soviet truck precariously held together with bits of string and wire. By the time all the passengers—both the legitimate and the 'yellow fish'—were settled, we were forty sitting on the cargo and mail bags at the rear, a compression in which legs and baggage became so entangled that it took some time for us all to dismount at tea-stops.

A short distance out of Chiu Ch'uan, we reached the lovely fortress of Chia Yü Kuan, western end of the Great Wall. The fortress, its outer walls and airy wooden-roofed gates in perfect condition, was completely empty of either people or buildings, although the inspection stalls for camels, outside, were intact.

After breakfast we drove on, and our road dramatically pierced the Great Wall itself. We were now 'outside the mouth' as the old expression calls this gateway to China, heading towards what most Chinese regard as a desolate land of exile.

A Shansi woman in our party, here for the first time to join her husband at the Ansi garrison, looked mournfully over the arid wastes we were crossing, and murmured again and again: 'Bitter! bitter!' Her dismay turned to horror when we reached the wretched though important little walled city of Ansi itself. The townspeople told us that this wind-swept city, consisting of dilapidated buildings sparsely set among tracts of mean fields, had several generations before been so devastated by Moslem uprisings that a new Ansi was built a few miles to the south-west. The *feng-shui*—meaning 'wind and water', the Chinese system of geomancy concerning that which is 'not seen and not grasped'—had been wrong from the start at the new town. Personal disasters had overtaken its inhabitants and the houses were 'always burning'. The people abandoned the ill-fated spot, our informants continued, leaving it to the wind-driven sands and returned to their old city, where our truck 'rested' for several days.

Throughout this trip we had halted several times an hour to repair the truck, which limped along a few feet at a time. It took over four travelling days to cover the two hundred odd miles which brought us from Chiu Ch'uan to within sight of Tun Huang city. Here we stopped altogether when a sand-storm of intense ferocity enveloped us. We passengers covered our heads with towels and climbed off the truck to sit miserably with our backs to the wind. Sand drifted to waist-height over the road and the truck tires spun helplessly. When the wind had abated a little, the mechanic went to the city to fetch diggers. These men worked their shovels furiously in front of the truck's wheels for the sand seemed to pile up again as soon as they had cleared a path. However, the truck inched on slowly, and after several hours we reached the city walls.

CHAPTER V

# End of the Highway: The City of Sands

Tun Huang's other name, still often used, is Sha Chow—the City of Sands. It is a highly descriptive name, more appropriate than Tun Huang—'Blazing Beacon'—for nowadays nothing much blazes at Tun Huang except the sun.

Tun Huang had been two decades ago a fairly prosperous oasis, before the road to southern Sinkiang fell into disuse. It grows excellent fruits and vegetables, and is the only Kansu oasis which produces cotton, used everywhere in China for padding winter clothes. Farming was entirely done by the most skilful irrigation, and it had 'never rained', an old pear-seller told me. This man complained bitterly of conditions in Tun Huang now that it was no longer on a main caravan road. A few trucks owned by the larger organizations came here, he said, to buy food for employees, because it was cheaper than elsewhere. A few caravans came, but not many like the old days. Here, as in Shantan, Tun Huang's present poverty and insignificance had preserved the lovely buildings of the city.

I stayed at the home of the garrison commander, a fine cavalry officer from Manchuria. He lent me one of the spirited regimental ponies and escorted me to the second site for which Tun Huang is famous—the beautiful Lake of the Crescent Moon, Yüeh Ya Ch'uan. The people of Tun Huang are greatly attached to both the Thousand Buddha Caves and Yüeh Ya Ch'uan, concerning which they have a saying: 'The hand of man made the caves, but Heaven made Yüeh Ya Ch'uan.'

We rode across fine sand into which the ponies sank above the hooves, and found, in the hollow of some lovely, very high dunes, a small spring-fed lake shaped like a crescent. Due to an oddity of the terrain, the wind blows drifting sand away from the lake so that it has not become choked as have the neglected wells of the desert. Between the horns of the crescent were the courtyards and temples of a charming temple, where visitors may remain for a meal or for weeks of meditation, as they prefer.

The sand is strange, consisting of minute grains of different colours, which the people here called 'five-coloured sand'. It gives an unearthly shimmering iridescence to the landscape, and at this hour of the day —late afternoon—it seemed every instant to change colour in the slanted rays of the setting sun. If you slide down the dunes—an irresistible sport—the sands give off a faint singing sound; if many people slide down together, it is quite loud, 'like thunder'.

Early the next day, I and a young cavalry officer who had come to Tun Huang on courier duty, set off on horseback for Ch'ien Fo Tung. Several armed soldiers accompanied us, one to act as a guide and the others to replace half a dozen men on guard duty at Ch'ien Fo

30. T'ang period wall painting: Cave 217 (P70). *See page* 94
Bodhisattva on panel south (left) of alcove

51. T'ang period wall painting: Cave 217 (P70). *See page* 93
Central panel of south wall, paradise scene. Lower portion of wall badly defaced within last thirty years

Tung, for the refractory Kazakhs, nomadic tribesmen of Sinkiang, were reported to be raiding.

As a pale pink dawn broke, we left the graceful willows and green fields of Tun Huang and entered the desert, which began precisely where irrigation ended. At first we followed a path beaten by the feet of pilgrims and their animals, but soon after we passed the earthen foundations of the 'ancient city', the path lost itself in the sand, and we had to rely on our guide to show us the way.

The last twelve miles of the journey lay ahead. The sun now burned in a brilliant blue sky, throwing into a violent contrast of purple shadow and golden light the immense dunes to the west. This range of sand-hills, thrown up by the fierce winds which sweep down on this region, stretches further west to the Desert of Lob, believed by the people here to be the haunt of horrible demons.

We rode slowly across the gentle slopes and hollows of the sand, fine as that at a beach, and once in the distance saw the flashing white tails of *huang yang*, small spotted deer. I was to see them again painted on many a wall of the caves.

After riding for several hours, I had hoped for the first sight of the Ch'ien Fo Tung oasis, which one of the soldiers told me was now only three *li*—about one mile—away. I could see in the distance only the jagged black peaks of the Nan Shan—the South Mountains, part of the range which separates China from Tibet—and more of this immense golden desert, its line broken by a watch-tower far ahead of us.

Our guide used that ambiguous expression which means either that 'we are arriving' or 'we have arrived'.

We jogged along, watching the tower which seemed with each step to grow larger, and I wondered why, if 'we were arriving', we could not see the green trees of Ch'ien Fo Tung.

When we reached the tower, I saw that our guide was right whichever he had meant, for our undulating road ended abruptly, and I saw that we were standing on the top of the cliff into which the caves are carved. The trees, concealed until now from our view, lay below at the foot of the cliff, forming a small plantation on the banks of a wide river bed through which a few streams trickled. The delicious green of these now full-grown trees planted by Abbot Wang was heightened by the tawny sand. Across the river bed, on the opposite bank, were scattered many small stupas and beyond their spires we could see the road used by carts and automobiles.

We dismounted to lead our ponies along the steep sandy path which ran diagonally down the cliff to a gate set in a wall. Over the gate it said *Mao Kao K'u*—the Cave of Unequalled Height—and hanging beside the gate was a clapperless bell. A notice nearby instructed us: 'If the gate is locked, strike the bell three times.' The gate, however, stood open so we walked in.

I felt as though I had stepped into one of the paradise scenes of the wall-paintings. We were hot, tired, thirsty and covered with dust. Beneath the poplars it was cool, the quiet broken by the musical blend of a stream, singing birds and the tinkling of little bells. Through the trees on our left I could see the walls and roof-tops of a pretty temple, the one, I learned, built by Abbot Wang. On our right were the caves, honeycombing the façade of the grey cliff. Where the cliff face had crumbled, we could look directly at the joyous colours of the chapels, a tantalizing spur to curiosity since I could not leave my horse. The guide had cautioned me sternly against allowing the thirsty animal to drink until it had cooled off.

As we followed the sandy path southward, I noticed the various wood and stucco structures fastened to the cliff like tidy wasps' nests. We passed a three-sided pagoda-like building which extended almost the height of the cliff. This, said the soldiers, was the *Chiu Ts'eng Lo*, the Nine Storey Building, of Abbot Wang; within was a colossal plaster Buddha 'tens of feet' high. From the turned-up corners of the orange roofs hung the little bells we had heard, swinging in the wind.

Our path skirted some tiny fields, cultivated in wheat and millet, and when we had almost reached the end of the oasis, perhaps three quarters of a mile, we found the compound of the Tun Huang Institute, where I was to stay.

The Institute's buildings, surrounded by a wall of pounded earth, were simple and attractive in the Kansu style—mud-brick plastered and white-washed, with roofs of grey tile. Set into the inner paths and walls of its courtyards were occasional beautifully moulded bricks decorated with animals and flowers, the first in high, the second in low relief. These had been taken, I learned, from the rubble of T'ang caves.

Mr. Ts'ang Shu-hung, an artist and the director of the Institute, was at this time in Nanking arranging an exhibition, in part to publicize the work of the Institute. His wife, however, received the cavalry officer, here for a day's leave, and myself kindly. We lunched in a courtyard where goslings ran between rows of brightly coloured dahlias and zinnias. In many another courtyard of the arid north-west I had seen such tiny gardens filled with flowers, lovingly tended.

Politeness demanded that I remain in the courtyard chatting and drinking tea, although the cliffs, towering above the compound walls, seem to pull like a magnet. Mrs. Ts'ang felt that after the fatigue of the morning's journey, we should rest, and beguiled the time by telling us of the present population of Ch'ien Fo Tung.

On this small oasis, less than a mile square, now lived about forty people, of whom three-fourths were attached in some capacity—as staff, students, workmen or servants—to the Tun Huang Institute. Besides the personnel of the Institute, who lived at the compound, two or three peasant families lived at Ch'ien Fo Tung in wattle huts. They cultivated the small fields we had seen but sold their produce elsewhere, so Mrs. Ts'ang said somewhat wryly. The Institute had to purchase all food at Tun Huang, transporting it to Ch'ien Fo Tung by horse, or more rarely, by truck.

There were three temples on the banks of the oasis, but at this time only two had monks in residence. Next to the Institute compound was a small lamaist temple where the soldiers, here to protect Ch'ien Fo Tung from the Kazakhs, were billeted. The presiding lamaist monk, a Mongol, was much dismayed by them, for the troops, idle and bored, amused themselves in the evening by climbing the roof-tops and firing their rifles into the air. For his support, this monk relied largely on gifts from Tibetan and Mongol pilgrims, who sometimes spend the savings of a lifetime to journey to a distant shrine. One Mongol couple, wearing great sheep-skin coats despite the heat, were there with their baby during my visit.

32. T'ang period wall painting: Cave 217 (P70). *See page* 93
East (left) section of south wall

33. T'ang period wall painting: Cave 217 (P70). *See page* 93
West (right) section of south wall

## The 'T'ang Monk'

At the northern end of the oasis, where horse-back riders enter the site, was the Taoist temple I had seen, for Ch'ien Fo Tung is holy also to Taoists, whose religion has both influenced and borrowed much from Buddhism. A rather large establishment, this temple contained, besides halls for devotions, a number of kitchens and chambers for pilgrims who must bring their food and a certain amount of fuel—twigs or dried dung—with them. Two priests were in charge and part of their duty was to attend visitors, who stay here unless they have an introduction to the Tun Huang Institute. When I called on the monks later, I was interested to see that Abbot Wang had had painted on the walls episodes from the westward journey of the 'T'ang monk', Hsüan Tsang. A favourite subject, especially in the north-west, similar scenes, also taken from the legendary account and showing Hsüan Tsang with his assistants, Monkey and Pig, adorned the walls of other temples I had visited during the trip. Sometimes, instead of paintings, these fantastic and charming episodes were illustrated with tiny stucco figures, brightly painted, fastened to the walls.

Near this temple stood a rather modernistic building, the nearly completed museum of the Institute. Beside it was a fine stupa, said to be T'ang. The exhibits intended for the museum were housed in the main compound and included several inscribed stelae, taken for safe-keeping from the caves, and sixty rolls of manuscripts rediscovered in 1944. Mrs. Ts'ang did not know how these had been found. Perhaps they were part of the 'nest-egg' hidden by Wang when the Peking government demanded the remainder of the collection.

## End of the Highway: The City of Sands

Mrs. Ts'ang had pleasantly plied us with tea and information, besides showing us the several courtyards of the Institute's compound. She now asked if we were ready to be guided through the caves. The cavalry officer and I assented, and we set off with a servant who proudly swung a great bunch of iron keys. He was to unlock the verandah doors which guarded groups of caves and promised, with all the finesse of a side-show barker, that he would show each one of the four hundred and sixty chapels, not forgetting the 'sealed library' which had contained the manuscripts.

Just outside the compound gate, we crossed the stream on a plank-bridge. I noticed that the stream had shrunk considerably since earlier in the day. The servant said that this happened every afternoon but he did not know why, his tone of voice implying that the natural laws of physics did not apply to the Thousand Buddha Caves. We passed under the poplars and stood before the cliff, its face corrugated with cave-openings and verandahs, now outlined in white paint. On our right soared the Nine Storey Building, the view in Plate 5.

We climbed one of the stairways leading to the second level and found ourselves in the damaged ante-chapel of the first cave of this group.

On the remaining wall of this ante-chapel were painted two processions of tall bodhisattvas, facing each other on either side of the chapel entry. In their hands they bore trays of fruit and flowers, and stood in a pose which suggested they had halted their stately march for a moment, to bid the onlooker accompany them. The spaces between them were embellished with designs of lotus and arabesques. Exposed to the morning sun, the muted colours and outlines of these beautifully draped and jewelled figures were drawn on a background of palest yellow, perhaps the effect of sunlight on the original white, or perhaps intentional, since this was the background in some caves never reached by the sun.

We turned into the chapel itself, passing through a doorway, the upper corners of which were filled in to make of the passage an irregular hexagon. This doorway was several feet thick, and on each side were painted the portraits of several donors, whose purses had supplied the means to build this chapel. Facing towards the chapel, they were about two-thirds life-size, dressed in red robes, and appeared to be walking dignifiedly into the dim interior of the chapel.

One's impression on entering a chapel for the first time is indescribable, as though one had seen a vision. For a devout Buddhist, attaining this object after a long and trying journey, it must be an experience of intense exaltation. Outside, one's very eyeballs have been scorched by the glare; the colours, though ranging through many subtle gradations, are few: golden desert, green trees, the azure of the sky, an immense inverted bowl of porcelain over all.

Within the shadow-filled chapel it was cool. The eye was first caught by a large statue of Buddha opposite the entry, which appeared to brood silently over little clay dishes of incense left by recent worshippers. In the quiet of this semi-darkness, which seemed steadily to dissolve, the great figure with its maroon robes might have meditated here through uncounted ages, more than a mere statue of plaster with broken arms.

As we became accustomed to the subdued light, the scenes on the walls came into focus. Panels on either side showed majestic assemblies in which a central figure, serene and unmoving, was surrounded by a host of gracefully clothed and bejewelled attendants, the whole divine company seated above lotus pools. Over their heads were the symmetrical roof-tops of palaces and pavilions. No two panels were exactly alike yet each conveyed a luxuriant paradise of tropical bliss, where musicians played for delicately poised dancers and peacocks strolled across chequered marble courts.

From these panels, the eye travelled to engaging scenes, drawn at the side and below, of miniature horsemen in battle, farmers with their animals, and a multiplicity of vivid little men and women whose actions were confined within the walls of fantastic buildings or charming peaked mountains. From the harmony of the larger celestial beings and the lively animation of the small earth-dwellers one's view turned naturally upward towards the ceiling, sweeping past an elaborate pattern of small repeated Buddhas, each in the same seated pose but variously coloured, to the apex of the chapel: a small square of brilliant floral and geometric patterns, like an exquisite rug.

A low platform in the centre of the chapel showed where a dais containing once a large sculptured Buddha had stood. Around this, worshippers had passed clockwise in procession, 'following the course of the sun' and keeping always at their right the Buddha image.

The chapel floor, paved with square bricks each moulded with a lotus pattern in low relief (Plate 36) appeared as a lovely earth-coloured carpet overlaid with a faint green patina, perhaps the remnant of its original colours. From the chapel-entry around the central platform one could trace the circular path of

34. T'ang period: Cave 217 (P70). *See page* 93
Corner where north and east walls join. At extreme left of north wall, portion of paradise scene visible; to its right, the meditations of Queen Vaidēhī

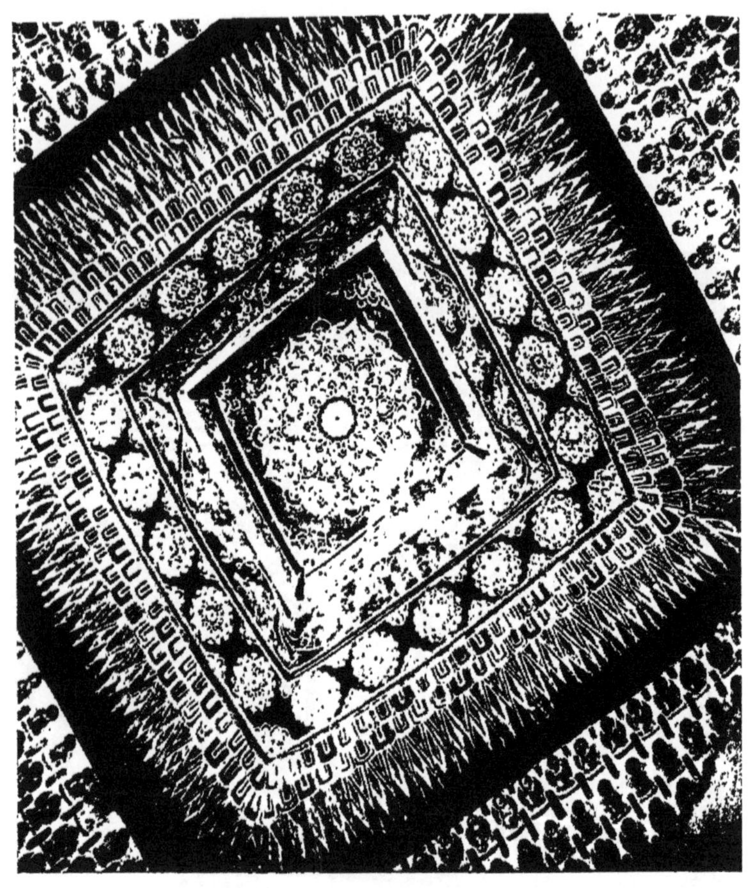

35. T'ang period. Cave 217 (P70). *See page* 93
Square panel of ceiling

the pilgrims' feet where the lotus-relief had been worn almost smooth.

The chapel seemed to be bathed in a green light, the effect of the colour most used in the paintings of the walls, a green so pure and tender it seemed to glow. Many other colours were here also—deep and light red, brown, black and white—but it was the green one saw first. We were to see its almost luminous beauty in many other chapels ascribed, like this one, to the T'ang dynasty, and which followed the general pattern of this.

When we reached a group of caves of another, quite different type, I said very honestly that I was tired and refused to move for half an hour. These chapels, I could see from the markers, were the earliest—Wei—dated to the fifth and sixth centuries. The lovely grey skin of many of the figures, modelled in black, the startling white outlines of eyes and nose, the dramatic juxtaposition of black, white, earth-red, blue and turquoise, captivated me as much as did the bold, vigorous line of the design (Plate 18).

In one chapel, the white background of the four oblique ceiling panels was covered with mythical beasts and flying creatures, almost revolving or vibrating with motion, and whose flowing garments seemed to be stirred by a swift wind. The paintings of these Wei caves, quite buoyant with their strong colours, differed almost violently from the refined elegance of our first chapel.

Our guide begged me to move on—the officer would, after all, leave the next morning—and led us up ladders and down steps, across verandahs and, crouching, through narrow entry-ways to the north end of the oasis. The entrances of some of the great chapels below ground level here were partially filled with sand, despite the efforts of the Tun Huang Institute. After sliding down the sand into these tremendous dark halls, we had to use flashlights and candles to see the wall-paintings and sculptures. From the point of view of size and richness of decoration, these chapels, built by the Chang and Ts'ao families (Plate 37), were perhaps the most impressive. The statues, like many we had seen, were appallingly ugly restorations with staring eyes, thick lips, and a boorish or merely stupid expression (such as that in Plate 46). Sometimes clumsy animals and garish warriors had been added to complete the Buddha's entourage. Part of this group of chapels had been restored under the direction of the monk Wang, whose single-minded devotion could not but touch the heart, although the results outraged the eye.

With a flourish, our guide led us to the chapel no. 162 (P 17)* which had contained the 'sealed library', hiding-place of the books and paintings of the monastic community for nine centuries. It turned out to be a small room, hollowed into the right-hand or north wall, now open and completely empty.

I had noticed with some amusement that outdoors the only signs with directions had instructed sightseers how to reach 'the library'. These, and a few notices tacked to the trees begging visitors to 'cherish these precious caves', were the only evidence at the oasis that indicated any tourist, as distinct from pilgrim, trade. Although Ch'ien Fo Tung was now a national monument, it retained the air of being primarily a living shrine rather than a museum of antiquities, and this

* This indicates Pelliot number, not plate No.

was partly due to the friendly simplicity of the Institute's personnel.

The first evening I sat with the art students attached to the Institute, gratefully joining them in a meal of 'dough-strings', an exact translation of the Chinese term which graphically describes the thick, half-raw noodles which are the main diet of the north-west. The students did not seem to mind in the least the brackish water, so bitter I had thought at first the cook was flavouring it.

After I had retired for the night into my cocoon-like sleeping bag laid on the mud platform—*k'ang*—assigned me, I heard the wind rustle the poplar leaves and set the roof bells jingling. From the temple next door came the chant of the priest joined to the throbbing drum of the evening ceremony. Then I could almost sense, as I was to feel many times in the caves themselves, the unseen spirits of the thousands—monks and nuns, pilgrims and donors, scholars and teachers, artists and craftsmen—who had laboured with love and piety to create these chapels, who had worshipped here, and whose presence still seemed to stand mute guard over this task of many generations.

CHAPTER VI

# Making pictures in the Four-storey Cliff

The days after that were full, for there was much—too much—to see and do. Each night I fell asleep instantly on the *k'ang*, hard as concrete and delicious as one of those air-and-rubber mattresses of American advertisements. My only interrupted night's sleep occurred when I assisted in a rather curious way at the birth of Mrs. Ts'ang's baby. My role was confined to singing lullabies and rocking the midwife's child, so that its harassed mother could give her undivided attention to the new arrival.

I had many plans for my visit. I wished to take some photographs, for I had brought with me as much film as the meagre markets of Peking supplied. I wanted to see—thoroughly—as many chapels as I could, and I hoped to learn also about the work of the Tun Huang Institute which had been so busy since 1943.

I arose early each day to take advantage of the eastern sun, which, for about two hours, casts additional light into the dim caves which are still intact, and noticed with pleasure that, in certain chapels, the first rays of

36. T'ang period. *See page* 68
Moulded lotus bricks which pave the floors of many T'ang chapels

37. T'ang period: Cave 61 (P117). *See page* 70

East (left) portion of south wall in a large, richly decorated chapel of the Chang-Ts'ao ascendancy at Tun Huang. Large portraits of donors painted on dado. It is not known when or why five cartouches were blacked in

58. T'ang period wall painting: Cave 156 (P17 *bis*), West wall
Panel over central alcove. 'Thousand eyes, thousand hands' Avalokitesvara

39. T'ang period wall painting: Cave 220 (P64). *See page* 93
South wall. One of the largest paradise paintings at Ch'ien Fo Tung, this covers the entire wall, approximately 20 feet long

the sun, penetrating the entry, lighted up for some moments the great central image.

During these early hours, I made most of the photographs of cave interiors, running from chapel to chapel according to a plan I had drawn up the night before. To my dismay, I was not able to draw on the experience of the distinguished scholars—Stein, Pelliot and Warner—who had come before. The books they had written were locked up in the Institute's library, I was told, the keys in Nanking with the director since he, according to Chinese custom, was personally responsible for these rare and expensive volumes.

For the first time on this trip I felt bitterly the lack of a good western department store. I had no tripod to hold the camera steady; the cable release had vanished *en route*. Worst of all, the delicate mechanism of my Rolleicord was full of dust from the sandstorm; I could hear it crunch when I turned the camera's dials.

I borrowed a wooden stool from the Institute on which to set the camera, propped to the correct angle with pebbles from the stream. I hoped desperately that the camera would not jiggle as I held the shutter open for long exposures. A sinisized tribesman from Yünnan province, who appears in two of the pictures, helped me greatly for the first two or three days by holding large sheets of white drawing paper before the cave entrances so that some extra light would be reflected on the walls. This boy, a student from the Baillie School at Shantan, was here to copy designs for their rug-weaving and silk-screen printing shops. Even those caves and statues which were exposed to the sun through cliff erosion had to be photographed before mid-afternoon, for the late shadows in this high, dry altitude were deep blue.

From the various personnel of the Institute, from several pamphlets published earlier in the year by that organization as well as by observation, I learned much about the work of the Tun Huang Institute. It is a record of hard work and idealism, carried out with the most scanty funds, a bright chapter in the sad story of disintegration and upheaval in China during the last years of the second World War and after.

This chapter really begins in 1941, when one Yü Yu-jen visited Ch'ien Fo Tung via the newly opened motor road. He had been shocked by the conditions of neglect he found there. Casual sightseers had carried off sculptures and wall fragments, besides leaving their autographs even more conspicuously than had been done through the centuries. Smoke from pious incense offerings, as well as the cooking fires of the Russian refugees, had blackened many walls. A recent hazard were the local sulphur matches cigarette-smokers struck against the plaster, since both match-boxes and the cloth shoes of visitors were useless for igniting these miniature explosives. The sun was fading many exposed frescoes.

In some manner, many standing frescoes had been damaged also. Large portions, quite clear in the Pelliot photographs, were almost obliterated within the next thirty years, as a comparison of Plates 32 and 33 with the Pelliot plates CXXI and CXX respectively, will show. Since much of this damage has occurred at knee and shoulder level it may have been caused by visitors rubbing their garments accidentally against the dry pigment, which comes off when it is touched.

## Damage and Deterioration

As has been noted, the gradual crumbling over many years of the cliff face has damaged or completely ruined many ante-chapels, besides dissecting or destroying a number of chapels (Plate 7). Some frescoes had fallen off the walls or were peeling away, while others had been ruthlessly gouged by Abbot Wang when he knocked holes in the walls between chapels to form connecting passages.

Most of the superstructures, which had simulated free-standing buildings and had formed the outer half of many ante-chapels, and verandahs, which had served to connect groups of chapels, had long since disappeared so that a number of caves on the higher levels were virtually inaccessible. The Russian refugees had let themselves down by ropes from the cliff top to investigate them.

Some caves at or below ground level had gradually been filled, partially or completely, with drift sand which, in this area, if not kept constantly cleared will rapidly obliterate all in its path, from walled cities to a horse's hoofprint. Many caves contained rubble and debris from crumbling frescoes and sculptures as well as sand; some were later found to have human bones and other things in them.

Besides this more or less haphazard deterioration, there seemed to have been systematic vandalism of at least two kinds. One was apparently iconoclastic. Persons unknown, perhaps Mohammedans, had lopped off the heads of larger sculptures, as the fact that a great many of these had restored heads showed (Plate 9). Other heads had merely been mutilated. Many lesser figures, oddly enough, such as bodhisattvas, warrior-guardians and arhāts, were more or less intact, as those of Plates 41 and 42.

## Making Pictures in the Four-storey Cliff

Another type of methodical damage was caused by thieves, who had gouged from the wall-paintings and sculptures gold and silver leaf. This was sometimes used from the earliest periods for the ornaments of deities and attendants, and, from T'ang, occasionally for the faces and torsos of the figures in the paradise paintings also. It was sad to come upon a graceful group and find each head a dust-coloured smudge of the underlying plaster.

The devoted guardian Wang had died ten years before. The monks in charge of Ch'ien Fo Tung after him, though faithfully serving pilgrims, were more interested in the 'living' trees he had planted than the 'dead' caves he had tried to restore to former grandeur.

When Yü Yu-jen returned to the seat of the war-time government at Chunking, he enlisted the support of a number of prominent artists and scholars, who petitioned the Supreme Defence Council of the government to set up an official organization to protect the caves. This body would at once repair and care for the caves, and also aid scholars and artists in research. After certain preparations, the Ministry of Education formally opened the Tun Huang National Art Research Institute, to translate its official title, on January 1, 1943 at Ch'ien Fo Tung.

One of the new organization's first tasks was to construct a wall around the oasis and section of cliff where the cave-temples were situated, so that the coming and going of visitors might be somewhat controlled. Another was to build a compound for its personnel. The tedious and exacting business of cleaning out, repairing and making the caves accessible, as well as classifying them, could then be undertaken.

40. T'ang period wall painting: Cave 220 (P64). *See page* 95
Detail. Musicians on west (left) side of north wall, balancing a similar group on the right

41. T'ang period: Cave 458 (P118/R). *See page* 75
Painted Clay sculpture, with minor restorations. Buddha with attendants. Figures face east

## Rediscovered Chapels

Falling and loosened frescoes were reinforced with plaster as were the passageways made by Wang. Images which had fallen over or dropped from the walls were repaired when the pieces could be found, although they were never repainted or restored by the Institute; its aim was rather to conserve what existed than make changes. The cleaning of sand and debris from the chapels was done by men hired from Tun Huang, and, by 1948, some 320 chapels had been cleaned and repaired. It is interesting that the Institute's plan and elevation published in 1948 shows the ground level to be several feet lower than in the Pelliot plan, a monument to the Institute's hard work.

During this work, a number of chapels were rediscovered, such as a group of seven sealed by the platform of the building numbered 119 in the Pelliot plan. It was sometimes found also that what appeared from the outside to be a single entry-way on a higher level was actually a porch window, and that within there were sometimes more than one chapel. Professor Pelliot in his published plan numbered slightly over 370 caves. The Institute's count by 1948 was 460; the disparity is not only due to rediscovered chapels, but to a different system of numbering.

In order to make every chapel accessible, the Institute built connecting verandahs and stairways, made of wood and the ubiquitous plaster, neatly outlined in whitewash (Plate 6). A few of the higher, more isolated chapels were to be reached by ladders, set against holes in the chapel floor. Climbing into a chapel through a hole in the floor was, though unintentionally, a charming way to enter it. The visitor seemed to enact ceremonially the ascent to one of those heavens pictured on the wall, just as the new-born souls in the paintings themselves emerged into the Western Heaven through the open cup of a mud-born lotus flower.

A wooden door, which could be locked, was placed before the entrance to each verandah, and, in some cases, before individual chapels. Inscriptions over these doors, which were enormously expensive because suitable wood is scarce here, stated that their cost had been subscribed by such-and-such an organization or guild. These latter-day donors had not left their portraits however, nor—more appropriate to the times—their photographs.

A new system of numbering the chapels, the third, was devised by the Institute, inevitably more complete than those of Professor Pelliot and Mr. Chang Ta-ch'ien, a noted artist and one responsible for the founding of the Institute.

All three numbers, those of Pelliot and Chang preceded respectively by P and C, were painted in the chapels, together with the dynastic date, and numbers were also given to individual shrines, when they either stood detached from any cave or were all that remained of a partially destroyed one. The markers of over forty chapels, considered 'representative' or outstanding, historically or artistically, were starred. It had been planned also to place a notice in each cave which would give all pertinent information concerning the exact date, if given in the dedicatory inscriptions, and any other data that would instruct scholars and visitors, but this had not been done up to the time of my trip.

It seemed a pity that the numbered markers should have been painted so conspicuously, for they certainly marred the appearance of the caves. Possibly the expense of making wooden markers which might have been placed unobtrusively in or near the chapels—or the risk of their being carried off for fuel—was the reason.

Mr. Chang's system, though not without merit, is rarely used. His lasting contribution will undoubtedly be his share in the setting up of the Institute, in the fine copies he made of wall-paintings which created much Chinese interest in the site, and in a book of line drawings of details published in 1942 in Chengtu, Szechuan.

It seems possible that the complete and sensible system of numbering designed by the Tun Huang Institute will eventually be adopted by scholars all over the world. It is already used in the few recent publications concerning the caves. If and when the results of the researches made by Chinese artists and scholars, who have spent extended periods at the caves since the founding of the Institute, are published, they will probably also use the new system. Little of this material, collected in the government archives at Nanking when the government returned there after the second World War, has been collated or published, owing no doubt to the profoundly disturbed condition of the country.

Another task of the Institute—and its principal project when I was there—was to supervise copies of the wall-paintings made by art students, who spent a year or more at Ch'ien Fo Tung on government scholarships. Through these, the government hoped, in time, to have a good record in colour of the most important panels and details of the frescoes. It is a commentary on the economic condition of China that it was cheaper to maintain artists to copy the frescoes than to have them photographed in colour. Actually the two methods are mutually complementary and both are necessary here. It would be almost impossible for a contemporary artist, grounded as a rule neither in traditional painting nor in Buddhism, to completely capture the spirit, the line and the balance of the larger wall-paintings, especially those of religious content. For these, and wherever photographically possible, the camera would be best used. However, there were many details—for instance, the architecture, musical instruments, carts, ships, costumes—which are best copied, and thus isolated and enlarged, for those who wish to study China's past material civilization. In addition, it would be impossible with the best wide-angle lens to photograph certain panels in the format of a hand scroll; to reproduce these as a unit copying would be the best way.

There were in residence, at the time of my visit, a dozen students—both men and women—who worked six days a week making the copies. They used powdered mineral and other colours, mixed with water, on special paper imported from Chengtu, capital of Szechuan province and a famous paper-making centre. The best copies, showing that dexterity and painstaking attention to detail for which the Chinese are famous, were very accurate, although this was not true of all.

Mr. Ts'ang Shu-hung, the director of the Institute, had taken to Nanking and Shanghai that summer a number of the best copies, which were exhibited with photographs made by a group under Mr. Lo Chi-mei of the Central News Agency. The exhibitions were held under the sponsorship of the Ministry of Education and, arranged in twenty-seven categories, such as paradise

42. T'ang period: Cave 159 (P21 *bis*), West wall. *See page* 75
Arhats, bodhisattvas, warrior-guardians of alcove

43. T'ang period wall painting: Cave 159 (P21 *bis*), West wall. *See page* 93
Panel at north (right) of alcove. Mañjusrī on the lion vehicle

scenes, borders and aureoles, demons, vehicles, and so on, created great interest in the two cities. This was the first time the general public of any city in the world had been able to gain an idea of the beautiful colours of the wall-paintings, or indeed of the actual contents of the chapels, since the published monochrome photographs are not generally available, through scarcity and expense.

One aim of the exhibitions, as of the Tun Huang Institute itself, was expressed in the specially printed catalogue for the two showings. This was the hope that the study of these ancient paintings would 'infuse new life into contemporary Chinese paintings, now full of emptiness and precocity'. 'Then,' the catalogue continues, 'these exhibits will have had something to do with the Chinese artistic renaissance.' The Ministry of Education also presented a plan for the future: to send native and foreign artists to study at Ch'ien Fo Tung on government scholarships, but this plan, partly owing to the acceleration of the civil war, was never carried out.

Another stated aim was to supply scholars with new, unique study material, and to this end a selection of the copies was published in colour in Shanghai the next year under the title of *Tun Huang Tai Piao Tsoa Hsuan Chi* (Selections of Representative Works from Tun Huang).

The Chinese government had also hoped to extend its protection to some of the other groups of cave-chapels in Kansu, either through the Tun Huang Institute or similar organizations. It arranged trips to the nearest of these for its art students but, through lack of money, the Institute had not made any repairs in them.

# Making Pictures in the Four-storey Cliff

After I had been at Ch'ien Fo Tung for two or three days, I found that my visit might be cut short. I had expected to have several weeks to wander through the various chapels, to observe, study and, above all, enjoy them, an absorbing occupation which could take years. Unfortunately, a messenger rode in from Tun Huang carrying, as though it were a jewel, a telegram which had been faithfully relayed up the road. The slightly garbled wording of this bit of yellow paper made it pressing that I return to Lanchow within two weeks. At the rate I had progressed to Tun Huang—seventeen days—I should have left immediately, which I had no intention of doing.

As a now experienced truck-traveller, I was sure I could cover the distance to Lanchow in a week, once I had found some way of reaching Ansi and the main highway. I sent word back to the garrison commander, respectfully asking that he let me know of any trucks departing Tun Huang after I had spent seven days at the caves. My duty done, I hoped fervently that no conveyance would materialize for a month, a wish that could come true at Tun Huang, for the 'regular car' was somewhat misnamed and even the horse-drawn carts, which took four days to reach Ansi, did not leave often. As it happened, I left ten days after my arrival on the battered truck, delayed by urgent need of repairs, which had first carried me to Tun Huang.

CHAPTER VII

# Paradise in two Dimensions: the Wall-Paintings

I returned often to the Wei chapels I had found so enchanting during our break-neck tour of the first day. This group of twenty-three chapels, I was told, was usually the favourite of occidental visitors, of whom some two dozen visited Ch'ien Fo Tung that year, the greatest number in its history. Incidentally, because of this 'influx' of both westerners and also Chinese officials and scholars, coming as tourists rather than as pilgrims, the Tun Huang Institute planned—and actually built the following year—a guest-house, which to date has probably sheltered few, if any, western visitors.

Such westerners as were grounded in 'modern art' found the earliest wall-paintings appealing, for both Wei and contemporary western painting occupy themselves with colour, line and texture. The strength and apparent spontaneity of the Wei frescoes delight most westerners because they are not repelled, like many Chinese visitors, by the Wei distortions and frequent seeming disorderliness.

# Paradise in two Dimensions

It has not been fully examined how many later chapels contain, under later paintings, frescoes of the Wei period, but it is suspected that there are quite a large number. The Tun Huang Institute has carefully peeled away a portion of the newer plaster in one chapel to reveal the original Wei paintings. Here the colours remain presumably as they were laid on, unchanged by time and oxygen.

The grey flesh tones of the Wei figures I so admired were pink here, modelled in a deep rose which had later turned black. The original pinks were in varying shades which oxidized not only to grey but to differing tones of brown, from *café au lait* to a deep chocolate tinged with grey. The dramatic white outlines of the eyes and nose appeared earlier as highlights, afterwards thrown into sharp relief by the oxidation of the original flesh colours (for examples, see Plates 12—18). The rosy flesh of long ago may have been closer to nature, but it was not as charming or striking, I thought, as the figures stood to-day, after natural chemistry had changed—and perhaps improved—them.

These chemical changes also demonstrated vividly the 'formula' by which the Wei figures were drawn, since oxidation has caused the outlines and shading to stand out in almost diagrammatic form. The heads are usually—though by no means always—drawn three-quarter face. The oval of the head is set on a neck containing one or more creases. Two ellipses form the breasts, joined to the ellipse of the belly by the gracefully curved lines of a slim waist. A necklace may reach exactly to the navel, and a loose stole, often striped, float from the shoulders as though borne by an upward-rising breeze. A loin cloth or skirt and, frequently, an elaborate headdress complete the garments of these lightly clad figures. Arms and legs, usually elongated, are delineated with a few deft strokes, the curves of finger and toe joints exaggerated. The hands and often the feet are drawn very gracefully. In Plates 12, 16 and 18, one may easily trace the elements of this 'formula' which has been used with many variations, while in the upper portion of Plate 17, and in almost all 'Thousand Buddha' designs of this period, the figures have oxidized almost to caricatures.

The other Wei colours which I could compare with the small portion of recently exposed wall appeared to have changed very little, if at all, for the extreme aridity of the atmosphere here and the lack of sun in many chapels act as excellent preservatives. Even the pigments of those frescoes exposed to the sun, perhaps for centuries, still retained something of their original colour.

The principal subjects of the Wei chapels are *jātaka* stories of Buddha's former incarnations, scenes from his last birth, and deities, alone or in groups. The first type is represented by Plate 16, where, reborn as King of the Sibis, Buddha offers his own flesh to a falcon that he may redeem a dove. The second type, less frequent, is possibly shown by Plate 14 which may represent the assault by Māra, with animals and demons converging on the unperturbed Buddha. One of the most commonly depicted events of Buddha's life is the *paranirvāna*, where Buddha is shown lying on his right side, surrounded by mourners. The third main subject of the Wei caves—paintings of deities and their attendants—may be seen in Plate 12.

The *apsara*—celestial maidens or angels—in the

Wei frescoes were especially delightful (Plate 16). They float delicately above the head of the Buddha in graceful, though completely un-human postures, their hands sometimes clasped or outstretched. Elsewhere they hold musical instruments, some of which are still used today, such as the flute and the *sheng*, a sort of mouth organ. With their airborne scarves and skirts ending like wings or flames, they emphasized the 'flying quality' of the Wei paintings, as a Chinese critic calls it.

All the Wei ceilings, often differing from each other in both shape and decoration, were striking and usually beautiful. The four slanted ceiling panels of Cave 249 (P 101) shown in Plate 11 were especially vivid with their gryphons, headless human torsos with feline paws, strange eleven-headed monsters, banners and mounted men, all in apparently violent motion, accentuated by strong cobalts and blacks painted on a white background. On the rounded ceiling of Cave 272 (P 118/J) in the frontispiece were sprightly *apsara*; the rarely found circular alcove contained a compass-like pattern on a deep earth-red background, on which were also laid painted figures in turquoise skirts and a shower of small blossoms. Elsewhere were intricate floral designs ranged on each side of a V-shaped ceiling. On the ceilings of this period—and later—the Chinese genius seemed to have ignored the influence of the 'western regions' or else had completely absorbed and transmuted it.

Cave 254 (P 105), a richly painted chapel of which the dominant colour is blue, shows a pageant of animal scenes from the *jātaka* tales, drawn with the spirited vivacity of all the animals of the Wei paintings. Plate

14 from this chapel gives the impression of a mêlée of human figures, animals and supernatural beings through which, on the Buddha's left, can be traced a tiger, while on his right three lively monkeys can be seen encircling a small white elephant. Deer are a favourite animal subject also, sacred to Buddhist literature, for which live models could be found in the surrounding desert. Pictured near the deer and elsewhere are often stylized cone-shaped mountains painted in many different colours (Plates 11, 15).

Certain decorative motifs are interesting because they simulate architectural details, some of which are found in the carving of the Central Asian rock-cut chapels. One of these is the 'lantern roof' of Plate 11, where the squares-within-squares are painted on the ceiling, since the brittle conglomerate of the Ch'ien Fo Tung cliff prevented their being carved out in detail. In addition, this 'lantern ceiling' pattern is also used as a decorative device, without architectural meaning, in at least two types of chapels. On certain early V-shaped ceilings, it is used as a single row, contrasting with other patterns (Plate 19); on another type of ceiling, parallel at all points to the floor and surrounding an unexcavated portion of rock which forms the alcove for the central sculpture, the 'lantern' pattern is used as an all-over ceiling design.

Another such device, used in all periods of the wall-painting at Ch'ien Fo Tung, are the beam-ends painted along the upper and sometimes lower walls, which, as in Plates 12 and 47, seem almost to project into the chapel. In cave 254 (P 101) and some other chapels, brackets actually made of wood have been inserted into the corners where the ceiling joins the wall (Plate 15).

## Paradise in two Dimensions

One chapel of the Wei group, no. 285 (P 120/N), said to contain the earliest dated inscription of any cave—equivalent to A.D. 538—was quite unique, alike in colour and style, although it had much in common with the other Wei caves. Its shape was typical of the majority of chapels here—square with a pyramidal ceiling—but one felt, on entering it, that one had stepped into a large, richly decorated tent. The lower edge of each of the four oblique ceiling panels curved back to the wall, like a tent roof sagging under the weight of its heavy material. Ropes with bell-shaped ends resembling tassels were painted on the ceiling also, heightening the illusion.

Each of the four slanted ceiling panels, like those of chapel 249 (P 101) in Plate 11, were covered with mythical flying creatures (Plate 21). Here, however, they were finely drawn and coloured, combining animation with an elegance not found in the other, but lacking also the other's bold vigour and spirit. On the lower portions of the ceiling, where the line of the ceiling 'sagged', were painted small seated Buddhas over whose heads were charming miniature deer, trees and mountains (Plates 23 and 24). One interesting detail of this border is an archer taking aim at a tawny yak-like animal (Plate 24).

The walls of this chapel, equally fine, showed at least two distinctive styles of painting, each having its own colour scale. One, strongly resembling that type found in certain of the Central Asian frescoes, can be seen in Plate 22 where the wire-like line is sinuous and graceful. The colours are muted and refined, and the gold leaf, used for the ornaments of these figures, has fortunately escaped thieves, adding great lustre to the sweetness of these paintings. The other style, seen in Plates 23 and 24, shows charming, rather stiff figures arranged in symmetrical groups over the wall surface, elaborately dressed, painted in sombre and rich colours, a seeming translation into two dimensions of some of the bronze Wei figurines which, with their drapery falling to sharp points, have delighted so many in occidental museums.

One day, after spending several hours in this cave, one of my greatest photographic failures occurred. The lunch bell—a rusty tyre rim hit with a rock—had rung, and on my way to the Institute's dining room, I had paused by the Nine Storey Building. The enormous Buddha within is said to be between ninety and a hundred feet high. The immense feet of the image towered far above my head, and I peered upwards to see the face, for the figure is lit above through openings in each storey.

With its rather coarse face, this statue, last repaired and repainted in the thirties of this century, did not seem to me to have particular artistic merit. Yet its sheer immensity and the technical difficulties of making it at all were impressive, as I had already discovered when I had stood level with the face from an upper storey. This chapel, no. 96 (P 78), whether because of the virtuosity shown in its construction or a lingering sanctity because it may have been the first chapel excavated here, has received loving attention even when the other caves have been left to rot. Whether Lo Ts'un's cave or not, it is now the cave of 'unequalled height'.

As I stood in the semi-darkness of this lowest storey, a blue-gowned monk from the Taoist temple entered silently, and, apparently without seeing me, lit his incense and began to bow, reciting softly. The dramatic picture of the old man, incense smoke curling over his head, bent before the gigantic feet of the image, seemed the perfect symbol of Ch'ien Fo Tung as a 'shrine in being'. I opened my camera, but before I could focus, the monk had completed his devotions. He turned around to glare angrily out of one eye, and I saw that he was blind in the other.

Positively, almost insultingly, he refused to let me take his picture although I assured him that I would send copies, 'large ones' if he wished. He merely grimaced and said a 'hundred photographers' had promised such copies and he had never received one. 'I am an old man,' he went on, 'and I have no use for either photographers or for their "capture-the-image" boxes.' That ended that, and I turned my camera once again to the chapels and the site.

If a group of ninety-four chapels are correctly ascribed by the Tun Huang Institute to the short but important Sui period (A.D. 581–618), this was an intensively active time at Ch'ien Fo Tung. These chapels form a bridge between the volatile robustness of the Wei and the disciplined exuberance of the middle T'ang and later. Some Sui chapels are very similar to the Wei, while others differ only slightly from the early T'ang. The Sui ceilings, considered by some Chinese critics to be the finest and most varied at the site, show all the devices used in both Wei and T'ang.

An obvious variation from the Wei chapels was the changed palette of many caves of this group. While the pigments seemed to be similar, the emphasis had shifted to a striking predominant combination of red and black. Faces and bodies of the smaller figures, such as *apsara*, are painted black, a black similar to that used in the aureoles and borders, but which may possibly be due to oxidation, since many deities and donors have black faces also (Plate 26). The Sui designs, particularly of the aureoles painted behind sculptures, were bolder, less complicated and more showy than those of Wei (Plate 25). The groups of divinities begin to assume a more complex and rigid pattern (Plate 26), heralding the great T'ang compositions, and the slender, attenuated Wei deities become more solid and rounder, closer to those of T'ang.

The panel over the alcove of one chapel struck me because at first sight it looked like a Christian Eucharist. My own photograph of this unfortunately turned out badly, but it appears in Pelliot's plate CCLXXIV. Twelve little black figures were ranged on three sides of a pale object. At second view, I saw that this 'object' was a prone figure of Buddha, the head surrounded by a black halo, and that the 'disciples' were mourners, a familiar theme which appears in both paintings and sculptures at Ch'ien Fo Tung. I recall two such immense statues of Buddha lying on his right side; around one, the mourners, small newly-made plaster sculptures clothed in the garments of many nationalities; around the other, they were the original and unretouched, painted on the walls.

The few sculptures attributed by the Tun Huang Institute to this period were quite distinctive, lacking the gentle, madonna-like quality of some Wei statues (Plates 13 and 15), and the easy charm of others (Plate 20). Almost all were stiffly posed, their heads round and the necks rather elongated. On dead-white faces eyes were sharply outlined in black, with lips and forehead dots painted red. Although some of the Sui sculptures seem to have been recently repainted, the colouring follows that of the sculptures believed to be unretouched.

During the T'ang era, Ch'ien Fo Tung reflected the vitality and popularity of Buddhism in China. Tun Huang lay on the high road to the flourishing oasis-cities of Central Asia, a vital nerve-centre on the path across which people, goods and ideas flowed between the brilliant capital and the far-flung T'ang empire.

The vigorous experimentation of the Sui chapels crystallized and flowered into the ordered richness of the T'ang. The Tun Huang Institute has divided the T'ang dynasty into four periods for purposes of dating the chapels. These are: beginning 618–712; 'the apex' 713–765; middle 766–820; late 766–906

The T'ang chapels reveal many different styles of painting, yet nearly all have in common the large panels of the paradise scenes, the magnificent floral borders and designs, the side-scenes in the secular style and fine paintings of the bodhisattvas. Many contain the 'luminous' green already mentioned, although sometimes it has been mixed with blue to form a lovely iridescent colour, between green and turquoise, which, once seen, is unforgettable.

Certain of the paradise scenes are so cunningly painted that the onlooker, standing in the half-light, has the sensation of being himself half submerged in the lotus pools before the divinities. This illusion is especially strong in Cave 220 (P 64), where the whole left, or south, wall is covered with an intricately lavish scene, not divided like most into separate panels (Plate

39). The oblique lines of the balustrades and mosaic platforms of the dancers in the foreground add depth. The pigments of this extraordinarily fine and detailed wall-painting are, for some reason, flaking off, the more sad because this painting conveys, better than many, the verdant dwelling of the Enlightened, poised eternally under showers of falling blossoms.

Another T'ang chapel, no. 159 (P 21 *bis*) delighted one by the rich elegance and subdued note of its colours, and also because of its pleasing, almost unrestored sculptures (Plate 44). Their draperies, as though of printed cloth, were painted with the same tones, predominantly green, used on the walls. The central Buddha of the alcove was gone, yet the empty space before the aureole was oddly eloquent, reminding one of the ancient device of not representing Buddha in human form. I was grateful that no new sculpture had been placed here as in chapel 231 (P 81) where the west wall, containing the alcove, was so similar to this that it might have been painted by the same artists (see Pelliot Plates CLXV–CLXVII). The ceiling of the alcove, above the heads of the images, was a rich mosaic of flowers in green (Plate 45) flanked by two elaborate panels: Mañjūsri astride a lion (Plate 43), balanced on the left by Samantabhādra on his vehicle, the elephant. This chapel would have been a perfect example of its type had not half the ceiling plaster fallen away. Its ceiling is typical of many chapels of this period, where the 'lantern roof' pattern has been replaced by floral and other designs.

Another cave, ascribed to the late T'ang period, no. 217 (P 70) attracted by the different spirit shown in its drawing and colours, equally vivid and strong (Plates 27–35). The delicate green of chapel 159 (P 21 *bis*) is replaced by shades of dark green, olive and lime, juxtaposed with reds and other richly contrasting colours. The multicoloured cloud scrolls, dividing the many scenes of the wall from each other or framing them, are a spirited device for creating 'cells of space' in which these scenes may be painted. Other means have been used throughout the wall-paintings to create these frames or 'space cells', as they have been called; sometimes courtyard walls and mountain ranges have been used as well as vertical, horizontal and oblique lines. In almost every case, these have been drawn so skilfully that they enhance the beauty and interest of the whole composition.

The type of bodhisattva which Chinese artists had developed by the T'ang dynasty—posed with elegance and reserve, adorned with elaborate jewellery, and wearing over outthrust hips a clinging skirt—is found in many chapels, where it is often painted on the panels on either side of the alcove (Plates 29 and 30). The faces and bodies of the two figures in these photographs, like those in many T'ang paintings and sculptures here, have oxidized to a rich chocolate brown, or so chemical analyses made at the Fogg Museum at Harvard University seem to indicate. It appears that the pigment used contained red lead, so that those figures, which seem so beautiful now, were once painted in shades of pink. The lotus in the hand of the bodhisattva in Plate 29 is blue, a colour relatively little used at this period at Ch'ien Fo Tung.

The noble yet tender paintings of the central deities of the paradise scenes could not fail to enthrall the observer, yet within these panels were many charming details, such as the babies, symbolizing new-born souls, emerging from lotus flowers into the ravishing delights of heaven. I was especially taken with the groups of musicians in the foreground, as well as by the one, or sometimes two, dancers for whom they performed. These dancers, poised forever halfway through a celestial pirouette, were very like the lovely T'ang *apsara* who hovered overhead or emerged in swift upward flight from many-coloured clouds. There was, in these paintings of musicians and dancers, something so spirited and graceful that I was not surprised to learn that, during the T'ang dynasty, Indian music and dancing were very popular in China, and that troupes of Indian and Indian-taught Central Asian performers visited the court. It is possible then that the artists of Ch'ien Fo Tung based these paintings on scenes of music and dancing they had actually seen, if such troupes stopped at Tun Huang (Plate 40).

The side-scenes of the T'ang paintings were an endless source of pleasure, for they were many and varied. I was particularly delighted with the hunting and battle scenes, which contained those fine horses for which T'ang art is noted. The desert over which I had ridden is beautifully depicted with washes of pink, lavender, beige, green and other colours blended into the subtle tones of the 'five-coloured sand' near Tun Huang. One was reminded that the desert is not monochrome, but filled with delicate colours for those who have eyes to see.

I lingered long over the little pictures of houses where women ground wheat in the courtyard and other, more athletic, ladies ascended the roof to lay something —fruits or twigs—to dry in the sun. Here in pleasing colours was a delightful pageant of the daily life of eleven centuries ago, its chronological remoteness made near because so many of the articles—carts, millstones, flails and so on—and even the gestures made in using them can be seen in rural China to-day.

The pictures of the donors were extremely interesting also. Some were simple, indicating by clothing the donors' sex, while others were detailed enough to enable one to people—in imagination—the chapels with men and women in brocades and silks.

The Tun Huang Institute dates a number of chapels to the period when the Chang and Ts'ao families ruled Tun Huang—an era between 850 and 1035 which overlaps the later T'ang, Five Dynasties and part of the Sung period, to the royal houses of which these families were sometimes bound by allegiance. These include the largest, most magnificent chapels at the site, a final burst of splendour before the tides of empire and trade receded, leaving Tun Huang far from the main routes. The great halls of this period—mostly at ground level towards the northern end of the oasis, as has been noted—are elaborately painted with beautiful shades of green, red and brown predominating. These chapels awe one by their sumptuous decoration and size and, unfortunately, because they are easily reached and are readily appreciated, have attracted the restorers. Where the wall paintings have been left untouched, their beauty emphasizes the ugliness and gaudiness of the new sculptures, of which many are Taoist. Only one sculpture from the Five Dynasties period remains, I was told, the small figure, presumably of a donor, unretouched and unrestored, wearing robes of delicate pink and blue. (Plate 46).

If one could plot a single line of development in the

44. T'ang period wall painting: Cave 159, (P21 *bis*). West wall *See page* 93
Detail of arhat, bodhisattva, and warrior-guardian on north (right) of alcove

45. T'ang period wall painting: Cave 159 (P21 *bis*). *See page* 95
Ceiling of alcove, north (right) portion

wall-paintings of Ch'ien Fo Tung, it would seem that the energy and verve of the Wei chapels, with their foreign and indigenous elements, had been harnessed and fused, through experiment and appropriation by the Chinese genius, into the exquisite jewel-like chapels of the T'ang period. The art then burst into the splendid luxuriance of the Chang-Ts'ao chapels, already containing the seeds of decay, to sink, exhausted, into the weary commonplace repetitions of the Sung-Hsi Hsia group.

In subject matter, general plan, and to some extent, the pigments, the Sung-Hsi Hsia chapels have much in common with the T'ang, and seem to be an extension of the more banal of that group. Yet the designs have lost vitality, their uninspired appearance accentuated by the poverty of the decoration, often done with stencilling. Even in the best of the paradise paintings of this time, there is a suggestion of the mechanical copying of a formula, not necessarily displeasing (Plate 47).

Cut off from the main artistic currents of the country, not easily reached from the capital, the painters of these chapels reflect little of the new developments in painting, especially of landscapes, which were to make the Sung period famous. In a few chapels, the new modes of conceiving landscapes are to be seen, such as the rediscovered portion in cave 27 (P 135 F) where a *Lung Wang Hai Hwei* (Meeting of the Dragon King of the Sea) is depicted, and also in the earlier 'panorama of Wu T'ai Shan' on the west wall of chapel 61 (P 117).

Yet the painting in these chapels is nearly always competent, and the ceilings, where the designs have become increasingly angular (Plate 48) are especially attractive. The colours are less varied, the effect less rich than in the T'ang chapels. Black, white and green predominate and, in some chapels, are almost the only colours used. However, if the hundred caves of the Sung-Hsi Hsia period are correctly dated by the Tun Huang Institute, it appears that the site attracted many benefactors. Perhaps it was significant that a great number of these chapels represent replastering and repainting of caves actually excavated earlier, since the worshippers of this period lacked both the zeal to excavate new cave-chapels and the taste to preserve the murals of the old ones.

The chapels made during the Mongol domination of China reveal a different, though not unrelated, type of religious painting, a kinship which might be described as that of first cousin once removed. In these chapels were to be found Tibetan models, which had been transmitted from India through Bengal and Nepal and which had also been influenced by China. Here one finds that the paradise scenes or as they are called in Chinese, *pien hsiang*, a more or less free representation based on the texts of sutras, have been replaced by paintings of *maṇḍala* in which the artist must follow strictly the esoteric rules for representation. One finds also the familiar themes of the many-armed gods clasping their consorts, and many other Tibetan motifs.

I was only able to see two of the nine chapels ascribed to the Yuan period by the Tun Huang Institute, for Mr. Ts'ang had carried the keys of the others with him. The most attractive panel, I thought, was one showing the 'thousand arm' Avalokitesvara, a graceful figure with a circle described about the head and torso. Within the circle, like a many-spoked wheel, were the 'thousand arms', an eye in the centre of each palm, symbolizing that Avalokitesvara unceasingly seeks those in distress and that each eye carries with it a merciful hand of help. The drawing of this panel, as in many others of this period, was balanced and meticulous, and here the colours were unusually pleasing—shades of green and varying tones of beige through brown to deep red.

Tun Huang, and with it Ch'ien Fo Tung, had before fallen under the domination of the Tibetans, from the mid-eighth to mid-ninth centuries, but their influence is not obvious in the wall-paintings or sculptures of the time. The Tibetan priests and patrons of that day had presumably been content to accept the type of art then prevailing at Ch'ien Fo Tung, as had the Tibetan-dominated kingdom of Hsi Hsia when it held power over Tun Huang.

It has been indicated that Ch'ien Fo Tung's history during the Ming dynasty in China is represented by a large blank and a hundred question marks, and that no evidence remains of any activity—either of restoration or repainting—during that time.

During the following dynasty, the Ch'ing,* two new chapels were reportedly excavated, and a number restored, a work that has recurred sporadically in all periods of Ch'ien Fo Tung's history and has continued, when enough pious people subscribed to it, at least to the founding of the Tun Huang Institute.

The Ch'ing chapels, both the new and restored, are in a class by themselves with their coarse, gaudy paintings and sculptures, decorated with bright red, orange, blue and green, covered with indiscriminate gilding.

* The last imperial dynasty in China, also called the Manchu dynasty, which ended in 1911.

One could not help but feel that taste and craftsmanship had declined sadly, as has the vitality of Chinese Buddhism itself although even to-day the strength of this faith is by no means dissipated. One often finds temples beautifully kept up by a devoted band of followers and one will meet priests of extraordinary character and intelligence, ornaments of their faith and their country. Among these are surely the forty priests of Chin Shan Sse, a famous temple in eastern China, who went to their death still chanting the scriptures, when flames consumed them and their temple in 1948.

The Ch'ing chapels of Ch'ien Fo Tung showed the horrors of hell filled with beings in torment, the malevolent gods of war and suicide, all painted with seeming relish. The atmosphere of these chapels, contrasted with those made before, is one of idolatry combined with banality, lacking paintings and images of competent workmanship. Yet, even such remnants of the traditions of the image-maker and temple-builder that these chapels reveal may soon be lost altogether. The present poverty of Kansu, the general lack of desire to build in the traditional style, force artisans trained in this work to seek other, more lucrative occupations and to dismiss their apprentices. In at least one city, I was told that it was impossible to find even one man who could paint, carve or build in the traditional manner.

Lying on the floors of many alcoves and chapels, awaiting repair, were many plaster statuettes. I was strongly tempted to carry off a pretty little bodhisattva, but each visitor of the Tun Huang Institute must now promise not to damage or remove anything from the chapels. This is a sensible request in view of broken or

46. Five Dynasties period: Cave 98 (P74), West wall. *See pages* 70, 96
The throne of this restored Buddha is typical of those found in the Chang-Ts'ao chapels. All figures are restorations except the donor at the Buddha's right, said to be the only Five Dynasties sculpture remaining at Ch'ien Fo Tung

47. Sung period wall painting: Cave 400 (P145/A), North wall. *See pages* 87, 97
Detail from paradise scene. Simulated beam-ends on lower wall

vanished sculptures which have fallen prey to would-be antique dealers who could find a ready and profitable market in the large cities of China. Other Buddhist rock-cut temples in China, notably Yün Kang and T'ien Lung Shan, have suffered more damage in the last three decades from the rapacity of collectors and curio-dealers,—both native and, during their occupation, Japanese—than during the more than fifteen centuries of their existence. Certain of Peking's curio-dealers offered many Yün Kang heads, most of them genuine, up to the time I left in 1949.

Within the last fifty years, fragments of the wall-paintings from Ch'ien Fo Tung might well have been added to the dealers' stocks, but the caves were saved from mass-plundering by their remoteness, by the technical difficulties of successfully removing and transporting frescoes, and perhaps more recently by the generally disturbed conditions in the antique market as a result of the second World War.

At least once early in this century, the best wall-paintings of Ch'ien Fo Tung were saved by sheer chance. The noted German archaeologist, Albert Von le Coq, then in Central Asia en route to Ch'ien Fo Tung, was summoned elsewhere by telegram. Von le Coq had successfully removed frescoes from cave-chapels in Central Asia, notably Turfan, some marches to the west of Tun Huang. Set up in Berlin, these wall fragments were destroyed by bombing during the second World War. It can be argued, in the case of these wall-paintings, that this was only a slightly quicker demolition than they would have suffered among the indifferent peoples where they had been.

The best wall-paintings of Ch'ien Fo Tung,

undoubtedly Von le Coq's object, were thus preserved *in situ* through this telegram of a fellow-explorer who, beset with apparently groundless fears, called Von le Coq to his side.

It is doubtful whether Von le Coq would have been able to carry away very many frescoes from Ch'ien Fo Tung. The almost wholly Muslim population of Turfan had not cared, but the local people of Kansu, which includes thousands of Buddhists who seem more attached to their religion than those in many parts of China, are deeply resentful when visitors arrive who might wish to desecrate their temples. Mildred Cable, an intrepid English missionary who travelled widely in Kansu and Sinkiang during the twenties and thirties, describes how she was not even aware of cave-chapels near eight Kansu towns until the villagers trusted her enough to show them. Sir Aurel Stein himself, in acquiring the manuscripts and paintings of the long-hidden library, worked in secret and at night because of the 'superstitions' of the Tun Huang inhabitants who, to this day, are by no means indifferent to what becomes of the Thousand Buddha Caves.

CHAPTER VIII

# Return to the Present

Chance, the dry atmosphere, inaccessibility and the sheer quantity of their number have combined—with other factors—to keep these chapels in a surprisingly good state of preservation. The original shape, the paintings on walls and ceilings of literally dozens of chapels, are virtually intact. In those caves not reached by the sun the glowing colours appear to remain unchanged, except for those pigments subject to oxidation. Even a fair number of the original sculptures are intact, although these, more than the frescoed walls, seem to have suffered man-made or natural destruction, perhaps because they are more fragile and easily removed. In any case, they appear to have been the first objects of restoration; wall-paintings generally have not been touched, at least in recent years, even when urgently in need of repair. Obviously immense damages have occurred at Ch'ien Fo Tung, but most visitors will be far more impressed by the abundance and richness of what remains.

Through force of circumstances, most westerners have gained their impression of the Thousand Buddha

Caves from Professor Pelliot's monumental collection of photographs. These were probably never intended to illustrate complete chapels as units, but were rather a systematic record of an aggregate of wall-paintings and sculptures. This is partly confirmed by the fact that few ceilings or adjoining walls were photographed, or so it appears from the published collection. Though not always clearly reproduced, these indispensable photographs, admirable for what they were intended, encourage the idea that Ch'ien Fo Tung is but a collection of wall-paintings interspersed with occasional original sculptures and a large number of new ones. Indeed, many travellers who actually visit the site describe it as an 'art gallery in the desert', which it is only in a limited sense.

Studying photographs, with their small scale, one tends to forget that each chapel was conceived as a whole, to which painting and sculpture were integrated. One must consider the proportions and relations of the wall-paintings and sculptures to each other and to the chapel as a unit, as well as the aims of the original artists and patrons, to understand the noble conception and exquisite artistry of the best chapels. Naturally, out of nearly five hundred, they cannot all be of equal quality; many are commonplace in the extreme. But some fifty are conceded by Chinese artists and scholars to be the work of masters, and ordinary visitors may feel this estimate is too low.

Although the two places of worship are dissimilar, it would be as ill-considered to judge the marvel of Chartres cathedral from monochrome photographs of the stained-glass windows and other details wrenched from context, although, by themselves, the windows, like the finest of the wall-paintings, can stand alone as works of art. Neither seen alone, however, will convey a true idea of the structure of which it is but a part.

Naturally, the architecture of the two cannot be compared. The stucco and wooden buildings which formerly covered the façade of Ch'ien Fo Tung's cliff were only a protective shell, often a necesssary part of the ante-chapels. The architecture of the chapels is inward, so to speak, and is, almost of necessity and perhaps also by design, simple in the extreme—consisting of but four walls and a vaulted ceiling—a plain setting for the jewels of the elaborate painting of walls and sculptures.

For the moment, it seems that the day a large number of western visitors can see these chapels for themselves must be postponed, for the communist government of China does not appear to favour the unrestricted travel of foreigners, especially if they are British or American. For many months, the world—or that part of the world that cared—wondered what would be the fate of Ch'ien Fo Tung under this most recent of the long line of rulers which has controlled Kansu.

Zealous party workers might have turned the site into a rest camp or meeting place, whitewashed the 'feudalistic and superstitious' paintings, and replaced them with portraits of the new heroes. Or the chapels might have been allowed to fall into the neglect which seems, no less than outright vandalism, to cause their deterioration. Thirdly, the government might give excellent care to the caves as 'national monuments'. In some localities, especially Peking, the policy was not only to preserve historical sites but also to finance and encourage archaeological research.

This policy did not always extend, at least when the new regime first came to power, to districts far from Peking, since regional commanders and civil authorities held wide local powers. In certain areas, reportedly among others in Shantung, many buildings and art objects were destroyed as distasteful 'relics of feudalism'. Much seemed to depend on the discretion and enlightenment of those in charge of particular regions.

This sort of wanton destruction was not to be the fate of Ch'ien Fo Tung, however. The communist government immediately extended official protection over the Tun Huang Institute and its work. Last year, the director and personnel received a unit citation for their work since the founding of the Institute eight years before.

One did not have to be clairvoyant to have guessed that events would take this course. What was surprising—although perhaps it should not have been—was that the art of Ch'ien Fo Tung was almost immediately pressed into the service of the government's propaganda.

At first, it might seem difficult to imagine how Buddhist wall-paintings could assume such a role. What happened was that a great exhibition of the artists' copies of the wall-paintings was staged at Peking where 'myriads of people' saw it. This exhibition was then sent to other cities of China and eventually to India. 'The art of Tun Huang,' so ran an official news article on the event, 'shows the harmonious relationship of the past several thousand years between the Indian, Chinese, and Burmese peoples. The exhibition will consolidate the great unity between the Asian peoples.' The Indian ambassador to China was one of the few from non-communist countries allowed to visit Ch'ien Fo Tung.

In China itself the wall-paintings were extolled as 'cultural relics created by the labouring people a thousand years ago, valuable relics inherited from our great ancestors'. The press explained that, thanks to the efforts of the new government, the 'cave-chapels were finally returned to the Chinese people after much robbery by American, French and Japanese imperialists'.

Recently the government greatly increased the funds allotted to the Tun Huang Institute so that it could purchase more equipment and increase its personnel, for 'in the Mao Tse-tung age, greater attention is being paid to research'.

Whether Ch'ien Fo Tung will remain an openly venerated shrine is a different matter. Official policy, while advocating religious tolerance, has been to discourage religious organizations of all types through exorbitantly high taxation on their property and sources of income, as well as by other means. Monks and nuns —Buddhist, Christian and Taoist—are urged to engage in 'productive work'; that is, they should quit the convents to become factory-workers, farmers, soldiers. Incense, paper spirit money and other things needed for religious ceremonies are prohibitively taxed, and an 'educational programme' of lectures, plays and pamphlets ridicules the 'shackling bonds' of the country's prevailing faiths. A possible exception may be the attitude towards China's Mohammedans, an estimated forty million, adherents of perhaps the most vital—or, in any case, politically the most important—religion in China to-day.

## Return to the Present

Whether the mass of the Chinese people will acquiesce is a subject which cannot be fully considered here, for no one can say how tenaciously the Chinese will cling to the traditions embodied in Buddhism, Taoism and what is loosely grouped under the terms of Confucianism and ancestor-worship. These have been the very fabric of Chinese social and spiritual life—a Chinese feels no contradiction in at once accepting all three—but there is some evidence that these ancient philosophies have been for many years losing their power, especially over the young, in the face of decades of political upheaval and a nadir in Chinese culture, both joined to the stunning impact of western ideas and technology.

These speculations ran through my mind the day I stood before the vulgar images of the newest caves. Mentally filing such thoughts away to ponder later, I did not stay in these chapels long, but ran back to those of Wei, Sui and T'ang, hoping to fix forever in my memory their shape, colour and design before I would have to leave Ch'ien Fo Tung.

One morning a soldier arrived with a pony for me. He said that a truck would leave Tun Huang the next morning and that a place had been reserved for me. This news threw my feelings into painful confusion. Had I been at Ch'ien Fo Tung, I wondered, for the ten days the calendar showed or, journeying back and forth across a bridge of time, had it been fifteen centuries? Then again it seemed that I had been at the sacred oasis for only the fraction of a second, the flicker of an eyelid, no longer than it took the wind to obliterate my footprint in the sand. I would have preferred to travel to Tun Huang riding this black pony, a journey where

48. Sung period wall painting: Cave 379 (P158/E). *See page* 97
Ceiling of chapel

49. The author photographed in a damaged Wei cave

the mind—held in suspension by the rhythmic plodding of horses' hooves and by the blinding light of the sun—could slowly adjust itself to the present.

Pony travel was out of the question. A mechanic had worked for three days to repair the Institute's truck—a weapon-carrier presented by the United States Office of Information at the end of the war—so that I might return to Tun Huang, whenever that might be, in comfort and style. Practically all the art students had declared a holiday, seizing this proposed expenditure of precious gasolene to taste the urban pleasures of Tun Huang. The pony was led back without its rider, and I returned in a truck which snorted its way across the desert in twenty-five minutes.

Time was similarly telescoped on my whole return trip to Lanchow. Roused at last to the urgency of meeting my obligations, I hurried down the road in five days, a record of sorts. When one truck could carry me no further, I 'yellow fished' on to another.

It was not too difficult. At the 'yellow-fish' stands I made such an odd appearance in this province of few occidentals that I could take my choice of trucks, after viewing them for soundness with a practised eye. When we reached Shantan, I found that the Baillie School planned to send, the next day, a truck expected to reach Lanchow the same evening. Since the driver of my previous truck had refused money for my fare, I presented him, by way of thanks, with a pair of live chickens hastily captured in the back courtyard by a shopkeeper.

The Baillie School truck actually made in one day this run of some three hundred miles from Shandan to Lanchow, a stupendous performance which shocked the truck-drivers of Lanchow. Our truck had been driven, for the roads and terrain, with enormous speed and had carried no load beyond a full complement of passengers and their luggage, an unheard-of extravagance in the northwest where trucks are loaded until the springs are straight. Our driver, however, claimed that we could have reached Lanchow several hours earlier had he not had to halt several times for me. By accident and intention, I had lightened my luggage on the westbound trip by leaving possessions at various points along the road—including a flashlight at the first caravanserai and a Han jar, bought and paid for, at an antique-dealer's in Wu Wei. Miserably poor themselves, the good people of the road had kept my things safely, for I would 'surely return some day for such valuable articles'.

At Lanchow, I relaxed in the comparative luxury of the Northwest House, official hotel of the city, where guests of a score of nationalities ate toast and melon jam under gaily coloured portraits of the war leaders—Stalin, Chiang, Churchill and Roosevelt. I tried to sort out my impressions but this would, in reality, take many months. Now, however, the journey was over, the dream of nine years fulfilled.

But when has this satisfied anyone? What is to be done after you have visited the place you hoped to see before you died? This was, in both senses of the word, a simple question and simply answered. Naturally, I continued to dream—of returning again, some day, somehow, to the Sacred Oasis.

# Bibliography

ALDRICH, RICHARD, *Tun Huang: Rise of the Kansu Port During the T'ang Dynasty*, unpublished Ph.D. thesis, University of Michigan, 1940.

BACHHOFER, L., *History of Chinese Art*, New York, 1946, pp. 95–100.

CABLE, MILDRED, *The Gobi Desert*, New York, 1944, pp. 42–51.

CH'ANG CHÜN, *Tun Huang Sui Pi*, Miscellaneous Notes on Tun Huang, written in 1742 and published 1937. *Tun Huang Tsa Ch'ao*, Stray Notes on Tun Huang, written in 1742 and published 1937.

CHANG TA-CH'IEN, *Ta Feng T'ang Lin Mo Tun Huang Pi Hwa, Ti I Chi*, Copies of details from the Tun Huang Wall Paintings, Ch'engtu, Szechuang, China, 1943.

CHINESE PUBLICATIONS, *Tun Huang I Chan Mu Lu*. Catalogue of the Tun Huang Exhibits, pub. by the Tun Huang Institute, Shanghai, 1948. *Tun Huang Mo Kao K'u Chih Lueh*. Brief History of the Tun Huang Caves, containing a plan and elevation dated August 1948, Shanghai, 1948. *Tun Huang Tai Piao Tsoa Hsuan Chi*. Selection of Representative Works from Tun Huang. Shanghai, 1949.

GILES, L., *Six Centuries at Tun Huang*, A Short Account of the Stein Collection of Chinese Mss. in the British Museum, London, 1944.

MATSUMOTO, E., *Tonka-ga no Kenkyu* (Wall Paintings of Tun Huang) Tokyo, 1937.

PARSONS, D., 'The Caves of the Thousand Buddhas', *Illustrated London News*, May 30, 1936, pp. 969–71.

PELLIOT, P., *Les Grottes de Touen-Houang*, Paris, 1920–1–4, 6 Vols.

# Bibliography

STEIN, SIR A., with LAURENCE BINYON, *The Thousand Buddhas: Ancient Buddhist Paintings from the Cave Temples of Tun Huang on the Western Frontier of China*. London, 1921. *On Central Asian Tracks*. London 1933.

WALEY, A., *A Catalogue of Paintings Recovered from Tun Huang . . . in the Museum of Central Asian Antiquities, Delhi*. London, 1931.

WARNER, L., *Buddhist Wall Paintings—A Study of a Ninth Century Grotto at Wan Fo Hsia*, Cambridge, 1928. *The Long Old Road in China*. New York, 1926.

# Index

# Index

Lightning Source UK Ltd.
Milton Keynes UK
UKHW021540281022
411262UK00007B/1063

9 780342 468164